D1175451

PRINCIPLES
of
POWER

SUNY series in

Women in Education

Margaret Grogan, editor

PRINCIPLES

of

POWER

Women Superintendents and the

Riddle of the Heart

C. Cryss Brunner

STATE UNIVERSITY OF NEW YORK PRESS

*LB2831.72
.B78
.2000*

Published by
STATE UNIVERSITY OF NEW YORK PRESS, ALBANY

© 2000 State University of New York

All rights reserved

Printed in the United States of America

No part of this book may be used or reproduced in any manner
whatsoever without written permission. No part of this book
may be stored in a retrieval system or transmitted in any form
or by any means including electronic, electrostatic, magnetic
tape, mechanical, photocopying, recording, or otherwise
without the prior permission in writing of the publisher.

For information, address State University of New York Press,
State University Plaza, Albany, NY 12246

Production, Laurie Searl
Marketing, Anne Valentine

Library of Congress Cataloging-in-Publication Data

Brunner, C. Cryss.
    Principles of power : women superintendents and the riddle of the heart / by C. Cryss
Brunner
        p.   cm.
    Includes bibliographical references and index.
    ISBN 0-7914-4569-0 (hc : alk. paper) — ISBN 0-7914-4570-4 (pbk. : alk. paper)
    1. Women school superintendents—United States.   2. Castaneda, Carlos, 1931–
I. Title.

LB2831.72.B78 2000
025.06'37—dc21   99-047840

10   9   8   7   6   5   4   3   2   1

To the book's 41 warriors:

the twelve women superintendents

and

the Assembly

FEB 1 3 2001

CONTENTS

PART THREE
MOTION: INTANGIBLES IN ACTION

FOREWORD

CHAROL SHAKESHAFT
Professor, Administration and Policy Studies
Hofstra University

Using as a framework Carlos Castaneda's (1981) system for teaching "warriors," C. Cryss Brunner makes sense of the work and lives of women superintendents as they seek to solve the "Riddle of the Heart." To understand the Riddle of the Heart, women must be able to simultaneously comprehend and use two different perceptions of the world: that which is and that which is becoming. To be able to solve this riddle, warriors develop a mind set and a discipline that allow them to get the best out of any conceivable situation. This book is the story of these warriors—twelve women superintendents—and how they have solved the "Riddle of the Heart."

Military, fighting, and battle metaphors aren't unusual in school administration. We talk about "being in the trenches," "fighting the good fight," and the "heat of the battle." Much of the early advice for school administrators was based upon the military model of leadership, with top-down orders and fighting readiness. For instance, in a recent issue of *The School Administrator*, the journal of the American Association of School Administrators, executive director Paul Houston called upon superintendents to be gentle warriors for children.

Warriors are often portrayed as solitary individuals—heroic, brilliant, alone in their leadership, and male. *The New Merriam-Webster Dictionary* goes so far as to define a warrior as a man engaged in warfare! Nevertheless, wild women archetypes exist in history and myth: amazons, gladiators, martial nuns, maenads, warrior queens, pirates, guerrillas, furies, and avenging goddesses. They are women who march forward armed with axes, swords, axes, bows, and spears.

Although less reliant on military images, women administrators have also used and been required to use battle models for leadership. Those who have had the courage to portray themselves differently have only recently come to be appreciated and honored for bringing an additional conceptualization to the role of educational leader.

Because it has been so difficult to legitimize female metaphors, I was at first put off by the warrior image. But as I read this fascinating study of twelve women superintendents, I came not only to understand the vision, but also to celebrate the characteristics of the warriors described in this book.

This is a book about superintendents and how they become and remain the chief executives of schools systems. More particularly it is about women superintendents, and how they sustain themselves, their dreams, and their constituencies in both difficult and rewarding times.

Women are warriors because they fight for children; they are also warriors because they have entered a domain where they are not wanted. Women have always been the minority of professionals holding formal administrative positions in schools. The history of school administration documents consistent male dominance in all positions except during a small span of time in which women were the slight majority of elementary principals in urban settings.

To understand women's current representation in administrative positions in schools and the history these women overcame, it might be helpful to remind ourselves how scarce women have been and still are in school administration. Women administrators have two battles to fight—the first as a warrior for children, but the second as a warrior for themselves. Women have not easily obtained positions of formal leadership in schools. The women portrayed in this book have not had easy access to the superintendency.

To illustrate how imbalanced the system still is, we can ask, "Are women and men represented in administrative roles in the same proportions as they exist in the population?" If we examine national public school data, the answer is clearly no. While women constitute 51 percent of the population and 51 percent of school children, the most recent national statistics on their representation in the school population indicate that women are 65 percent of teachers (83 percent of elementary and 54 percent of secondary teachers), 43 percent of the principals (52 percent of elementary and 26 percent of secondary principals), and 12 percent of the superintendents. Thus, women are overrepresented in teaching and in the elementary principalship in relation to their proportions in the population as a whole (65 percent of teachers, 52 percent of elementary principals versus 51 percent of the population) and underrepresented in the secondary principalship and the superintendency (26 percent of secondary principals and 12 percent of superintendents versus 51 percent of the population).

If we examine equality based upon the proportions in the profession, the question is: "Are women represented in administration in equal proportions to their representation in teaching?" The answer here is clearly no: 52 versus 83 percent in elementary schools; 26 versus 54 percent in secondary schools; and 12 versus 65 percent at the superintendent level. Females are overrepresented in teaching and underrepresented in administration.

While 15.9 percent of the U.S. population is Hispanic nonwhite or of African descent, 28 percent of students, 10.9 percent of public school teachers, 12.3 percent of public school principals, and 2.8 percent of superintendents are of African descent, non-Hispanic, or Hispanic (1990 U.S. Census Data; U.S. Department of Education, July 1996). The percentage of Asian and Pacific Islander principals is 1.5 and Native American principals are not plentiful enough to even warrant a report. None of these figures are available by both race and sex.

Although there are no comparable nationwide statistics that report administrative representation both by race and sex, a recent study by the District Superintendents Committee on Women and Minority Administrators in New York (1997) documents an increase in women and members of minority groups in all administrative positions. For women, these increases still do not bring women into administration in proportion in any of the positions to their numbers in teaching.

While minority elementary principals are roughly proportional to the percentage of minority elementary teachers, the percentages of minority secondary principals and superintendents are less than the proportion of teachers in New York school districts. However, administrative certification in New York State was acquired largely by women and members of minority groups. Women earned about two-thirds of all administrator certification and members of minority groups about one-third. This might mean that a growing number of women and minority members are gearing up to become school administrators. It might also mean that most majority males who are interested in becoming administrators already have certification. It certainly means that women and minority candidates are certified in much larger numbers than they are chosen for administrative positions.

With only 2.6 percent of New York State superintendents from minority groups, it is hard to understand much trend data. However, male and female minority school superintendents are evenly divided, as of June 1997, there were nine female and nine male minority superintendents in New York State. The New York data provide no support for the stereotype that minority women have it "made" and are a shoo-in for administrative positions.

The bottom line is that at the end of the twentieth century, the percentage of women superintendents is about the same as it was at the beginning of the twentieth century. The struggle for legitimacy and equality has consumed an entire century and, while taking women many places, it hasn't increased their representation in the superintendency.

To understand the historical context of women's struggle and the ebbs and flows of representation for women, it is useful to understand seven periods that affected women's representation in the superintendency:

1. The bureaucratization of schools, which promoted men into management in schools and limited the opportunities for women;
2. The early suffrage movement in the United States, which increased the number of women in school administration;
3. The movement for equal pay and the economic Depression of the 1930s, which decreased the number of women administrators;
4. The advent of World War II, which opened up jobs for women as men fought the war; and the post–World War II period, which prepared male teachers on the G.I. Bill, moving them into school administration;
5. The Cold War, which spiralled the country into a panic about the lack of preparation of students in math and science and increased the number of men teachers and administrators;
6. Societal expectations for women, which cast females into roles at odds with leadership and administration;
7. The most recent women's movement, which expanded career options for women and drew some women away from education.

Most of the women whose stories are told in *Principles of power: Women Superintendents and the Riddles of the Heart* came of professional age in the early stages of the most recent women's movement. Although it is part of a societal movement to advocate for equity and is responsible for opening doors for women, the most recent feminist movement has, paradoxically, brought subtle and sometimes not so subtle pressure on young women to reject teaching as a career while at the same time trying to open up the ranks of administrators to females. Especially during the past decade, young women, and particularly high achieving young women, have been discouraged from entering the profession of teaching, while women currently in teaching have not seen much of a change in the receptiveness of educational institutions to female administrators.

Although the Women's Liberation movement, beginning in the late 1960s, drew attention to the underrepresentation of women in traditional positions of leadership in the schools, very little change occurred for women in school administration during the 1960s and 1970s. The percentage of women in school administration in the 1980s was less than the percentage of women in 1905. However, during the late 1970s and up to the present, a number of activist approaches to encouraging women to enter school administration were begun. Efforts toward adding women to school administration have come through women's caucuses in professional organizations and separate women's administration organizations. Courses and workshops for women on how to succeed are common, as are recruitment efforts. While women are still not represented in proportion to their numbers in teaching in the late 1990s, the majority of students gaining certification in school administration are women, a trend that some believe will ensure women's equitable representation (Pounder 1994).

The women superintendents in this book were educated at a time when women were either unwelcome or tolerated in departments of educational administration. They moved into administration often as the first or only females in their positions. They dealt with barriers in their careers that were unknown to their male counterparts: societal beliefs in their inferiority; the need to choose between relationships and careers; weak or nonexistent support systems; expectations of their provision of maternal comfort and sacrifice; and overt and covert hostility.

Although there have not been many studies that directly connect the Civil Rights movement or affirmative action policies to the increase of women in school administration, there are reports that link the two. Women report that affirmative action pressure helped them because it created an opportunity for them to be interviewed. Sometimes that was all that was necessary. In addition, as affirmative action questions were raised in communities, the pressure to hire from unrepresented groups increased (Edson 1995). However, studies reflect the risks to women in school administration who become advocates for women and are seen as speaking affirmatively for women (Bell 1995; Schmuck 1995; Schmuck and Schubert 1995). The women in this study report the complexity of working for women and equity.

The relationship between affirmative action and women's participation in administration is complicated, with affirmative action being a factor that might have encouraged women to apply or encouraged committees to interview women they might not otherwise have heard from. However, there is little evidence that women have been hired because they are women; rather, the evidence indicates they are hired despite being women.

This book adds substantially to the literature on the superintendency as well as to the literature about women's leadership. By investigating women superintendents' place in schools from the perspective of those who have lived this role, C. Cryss Brunner helps us understand the complexities of the response to the often asked question: "Why are there so few women leaders?" Her extensive and continued work on the reasons that women are not in school administration in greater numbers has both aided understanding and prompted action. While there is considerable literature that helps readers understand the barriers to women seeking superintendencies, there is little beyond conjecture to help combat those barriers.

This book provides examples of successful actions that led to these women becoming both superintendents and successful advocates for children. Brunner adds to the research that helps explain the tradeoffs for women in administration and describes why the costs for women are sometimes more than the value of the position itself. The women in this book help to put into perspective the difficulty of balancing personal and family life with career and advancement.

The lives of women superintendents are brought to life as their stories are set within the Seven Principles of Power. These are principles that guide a warrior in her journey. Within this context, we learn how these women construct their gender in a male-dominated profession.

Many of these warrior principles and stories build the case that as women bring to administration practices that haven't existed before and that are necessary for reform, they do so in a disciplined and focused fashion. We see how the women superintendents in this book have continued to be democratic, caring, and reform minded against all odds and how, as warriors for children and for themselves, they have managed their professional and personal lives.

Apprentice warriors are taught to: choose and know the battleground; discard the unnecessary; consider carefully which battles to enter; relax and fear nothing; retreat when the odds are impossible; compress time; and never push oneself to the front.

When applied to women superintendents, we learn that for women, knowing the battleground means understanding who the "old boys" are and how to be better than the boys at "male" tasks while still projecting a kind and caring female image. In other words, these superintendents have to meet both role-related and gender-related expectations, even when the two are in conflict.

For many of the women, discarding the unnecessary means giving up friendships, family relationships, and any private identity for work— work that is an emotional as well as a career endeavor. In addition, these women put to rest the myths that women must act like men and that femininity is the same as sexuality.

These superintendents are thoughtful about their battles and when they engage, they do so passionately. The women focus on "simple" agendas and quiet persistence. Overwhelmingly, the agenda is the child; decisions and actions are guided by their effects on children.

While Castaneda advises warriors to take risks, risk taking is not highly regarded or practiced in school administration. However, women in administration are more, not less, likely than men to take risks and to rock the boat to accomplish their goals. Just entering a male-dominated profession takes courage, and the women in this book stand up time and again for those without power—the children.

These women also find ways to retreat, to revitalize, and to replenish their souls and their energies. A key to their success is knowing when to back off in order to restore themselves.

Compressing time—not wasting an instant—seems synonymous with "professional woman" to those of us who study the balancing act of women's lives. The warriors in this book are multitasked and able to accomplish many goals with one action.

Castaneda reminds us that warriors don't push themselves to the front. These women are nearly pure examples of how to orchestrate action through collaboration, inclusion, and involvement. They share power and understand that by sharing, everyone is stronger and no one is diminished. Much like the way the flame of a candle lights another candle without losing light, women move power to others while maintaining it themselves.

The Seven Principles of Power, when followed, create warriors who are emotionally involved in their work. While dedicated and serious, these women laugh at themselves. They also have learned not to hurry and to have great patience. Finally, the women superintendents have exceptional capacity to improvise.

An additional contribution of the stories in this book is that they provide a rich and descriptive storehouse of human female administrative behavior upon which to make sense of organizational, political, and individual behavior. These actions often challenge conventional notions of decision making in schools or theories that explain actions through benefit analysis. As a whole, the research reported in this book is building the field's understanding of the nature of gender in organizations. Gender theory is what is being constructed.

Finally, this study uses innovative and creative ways to weigh evidence and evaluate individual experience. Brunner begins with the stories of twelve women superintendents, supported by data about them from more than fifty associates and family members. She uses these stories as the foundation for an "assembly" experience, which allows others in similar roles to react, expand, and critique. Brunner reports both sets of data and demonstrates a way to think about the concept of "validity" in qualitative research.

This book is a pleasure to read and doesn't have to be engaged sequentially. Jumping right to chapter 5 (or other, later chapters) then circling back will be just as useful as a linear read. The women's stories are compelling, as is the idea of a disciplined and thoughtful set of principles to guide their journey. This is an inspirational and spiritual book and one that moves the knowledge base along.

ACKNOWLEDGMENTS

I have been blessed with many warrior guides and angels.
I am forever grateful to those I list and to those who remain unnamed.

Carlos Castaneda

Ray Olderman

John Brocksch

Clifton Conrad

Paul Bredeson

Paula Short

Patricia Nehm

Leslie D. Craft Sr.

Jean Craft

Janice Craft

Courtney Clark Meyer

Greg Meyer

Connie Hutchison

Judith Perkins

Priscilla Ross

Laurie Searl

Lois Patton

Paul Schumaker

Meredith Mountford

Betty Malen

Charol Shakeshaft

Karen Seashore Louis

W. Charles Read

THE WOMEN OF THE ASSEMBLY

Cora Acor

Dianne Beeler

Karen M. Beischel

Kathleen Cooke

Ruthann Faber

Gayle Frame

Janice Hardesty

Suzanne S. Hotter

Sarah Jerome

Jeanetta Kirkpatrick

Linda Kunelius

Barbara Lorkowski

Kathleen Martinsen

Mary B. Niebuhr

Barbara M. Noll

Judith Perkins

Karen Petric

Sally Sarnstrom

Rosa A. Smith

Cheryl H. Wilhoyte

(Some of the women wished to remain anonymous)

PART ONE

METAPHOR

INTANGIBLE INSIGHTS

Our work is to show . . . what we have received through our sudden knowings from story, from body, from dreams and journeys of all sorts.

—C. P. Estes, *Women Who Run with the Wolves*

So much of what we know arrives in mysterious vehicles—"sudden knowings from story, from body, from dreams. . . ." We live with the mystery of these intangible insights without much thought, often disregarding their importance and their usefulness. Perhaps this happens because of our inability to articulate and take action on shadow thoughts and ideas. But can we deny their importance? Can we deny that these moments of mystery are some of our most creative?

In my view, it is these moments of mysterious insight that hold promise for creating solutions to our deepest heartfelt problems. They are the moments of negative space, the millisecond of darkness between bursts of strobe light. If we can catch sight of these mysterious moments and somehow articulate them, I believe answers to questions about how to educate our children will take shape. Action will follow once these moments are articulated.

This section outlines the capturing of intangible data through the use of metaphor. Chapter 1, written by Raymond M. Olderman (an expert on "metaphor" and contemporary fiction), helps answer the question of how insight can be made into usable information. Chapter 2 describes the twelve women superintendents whose narratives and lives were examined for intangible insights—mysterious sudden knowings—through a research study that spanned several years. The methods and design of that study are outlined in the same chapter. It also describes a larger gathering of women administrators, called the Assembly, who met as a group to discuss Castaneda's Principles of Power. And finally, in Chapter 3 the archetype of the warrior is discussed in relationship to the women superintendents.

The primary goal of the book is to take "mystery" (intangible insight), articulate it through "metaphor," and reveal the "action" that results when mystery is articulated and acted upon. The book is consequently organized into three parts titled: "Mystery: Intangible Insights," "Metaphor: Articulating Intangibles," and "Motion: Intangibles in Action."

CHAPTER 1

MYSTERY AND METAPHOR

INTRODUCTION TO PART 1

RAYMOND M. OLDERMAN

Sometimes, data collected in the study of human behavior are too intangible for quantification. And yet they can be grasped. Intangible data, such as environment, atmosphere, and emotion contribute a different kind of insight into our behavior than does quantifiable data. We all know this. Intangible data only become a problem because we want data to give us more than insight. We want usable information, or to say it in another way, we want to make the intangible into something that's tangible enough to be usable. The question is, how does insight become usable information?

The answer goes like this: the insight is expressed in symbols and words that are metaphors describing the intangible-unsayable something experienced during the insight. The metaphors are the first step in transforming insights into systems. Systems "routinize the extraordinary," as Max Weber put it. They convert mystery into usable information.

Metaphors, then, are the primary tool for helping us turn insights into systems—intangible mysteries into usable information. I know this needs more explaining. But before I discuss metaphor, let me tell you what I'm trying to establish.

This book provides a system for understanding the field data gathered from the experiences of women superintendents of schools. The data are broad and complex so that they contain both quantifiable and intangible information. In order to communicate insights based on the intangible portion of her data, C. Cryss Brunner adapts a system to help turn these insights into useful information. The system she adapts is from the one described by Carlos Castaneda in his series of books that began in the late 1960s. Castaneda developed his system by interpreting the intangible world of Indian seers from Mexico. Brunner's use of Castaneda's system helps her turn the intangible dimension of her field study with women superintendents into a useful set of disciplines based on how these women coped with their experience, survived, and sometimes even prevailed.

Brunner achieves this successful adaptation of Castaneda's system by treating it as a metaphor—the first step to systematizing her intangible data. Castaneda's system provides disciplines for living "impeccably" in a world of multiple realities.

HOW CARLOS CASTANEDA'S SYSTEM SERVES AS A METAPHOR

The "Carlos Castaneda" who narrates the story in his books is an anthropologist gathering field data. He discovers a teacher and "seer" or sorcerer named Don Juan and together they move in mysterious ways through the landscapes, deserts, and mountains of Mexico. The narrator Carlos learns something about dealing with the terrifying multiplicities of the natural world. He learns disciplines to survive fruitfully in the rich, mysterious, nonordinary world of the seer. A seer is a kind of visionary— when we demystify these terms, we're talking about a person who can combine intuitive and rational clear-sightedness with disciplined systems for success and survival.

Now, suppose *you* are in an unusual world of threats and challenges, and you need disciplines to succeed and survive. You need to see clearly. But do you need to go to Mexico, trip around the desert and the mountains learning to "impeccably" practice the system's disciplines? Do you need to learn those disciplines in relationship to that nonordinary context of behavior? Or can you read the conditions for achieving the system's disciplines as metaphors, meaning you can be impeccable in the way you survive any challenging and demanding environment. Castaneda's system helped Brunner see a pattern in her intangible data that can be interpreted as a set of disciplines useful for women superintendents of school. *The way Castaneda's system presents the disciplines is metaphoric—the disciplines described by the metaphors correspond to something that already exists in the experience of successful women superintendents.* That's why the application works.

Now, back to the meaning of metaphor.

METAPHOR: OUR PRIMARY TOOL FOR GRASPING THE INTANGIBLE

Imagine that you've interviewed all the mid-level lawyers who were sucked into the Watergate scandal—the ones who, in the end, were bewildered by the key roles they played. As data, their stories capture a very important truth about the effects of power, illusion, and ambition on well-meaning "small fish" who wage war for ideals. Something about the mysterious meaning of Watergate's effect on Americans can be understood from grasping Herbert Porter, for example—small fish lawyer—crying at the Watergate Hearings and advising young believers to stay away from Washington. The tears, the breakdown of the "little guy," the hopeless bewilderment and trembling avowals of betrayal—taken together they are a metaphor that gives us insight into the unmeasurable results of a national scandal.

Metaphors are little tools. Their job is only to make initial order from chaos. Using a metaphor—as poet Wallace Stevens describes in his short poem "Anecdote of the Jar"—is like putting a jar in a wilderness as big as Tennessee. The formless, meaningless abundance of actuality will begin to arrange itself in relationship to that tiny jar. Physicist David Bohm would agree, but would add a caution: "Reality is inexhaustible and whatever we say a thing is, it is something more and also something different" (Bohm and Peat 1987, 210; see also 38 on metaphors). Metaphors can deceive us, but we are dependent on them as a basic resource for articulating insight.

METAPHORS DESCRIBE REAL PHENOMENA

Metaphors explain the *meaning* of intangible things by comparing them to tangible things. For example, when we say "love is a rose," we are saying that something about the actual rose helps us understand the intangible feel of love—love blooms like a rose; it responds to warmth and bears the fertile secret of reproduction; it is fragile, beautiful, sensual, alive, and perishes easily. Love is as real as a rose. But it's also something more, something different.

Both science and religion use metaphors to explain *relationships* between invisible phenomena. For example, subatomic waves/particles can be understood as metaphors for relationships between events in space/time. The metaphors describe the behavior patterns of invisible things and put names to the interactive building blocks of actuality. They are meant to be precise symbolic representations of relationships that exist in actuality.

Religious metaphors describe relationships between people and intangible ideals. The revelation of Jesus can be understood as a metaphor for the particular moment in history when love's importance made an impact on human consciousness. The metaphor "god is love" means not only that participating in love gives people contact with the divine, but that love is reality's prime mover.

SUCCESSFUL METAPHORS BECOME PART OF REALITY

Metaphors that successfully describe a phenomenon also become part of the reality they describe. Think about how an interpretation of "historical" events becomes part of history itself. For example, our traditional description of how we "won the west"—based on the metaphor of "the frontier as virgin territory"—is only one possible interpretation of the movement west in American history. But, for a long time we didn't realize our idea of the west was a frontier metaphor. We thought it was "the real story." In the 1970s new historical information—from Native Americans in particular—forced Americans to reexamine the metaphor of the frontier. We learned to separate the metaphor from the events it described— and from the "good guy/bad guy, pioneer/savage, settler/cowboy" models of behavior it fostered. Nonetheless, the metaphor of the frontier west as virgin territory had a real part in the evolution of our everyday social norms, so no matter how we look at it, the metaphor will always be somewhere there mixed up in the real story.

Except in matters of faith, where insights can come to earth without the intervening agency of human interpretation, all descriptions of intangible realities are metaphors. They participate in the actual but they are simply not identical with it. That's why the "realities" of history, physics, psychology, medicine, the Church, and other such systems keep changing—even though historians, scientists, and clerics periodically claim that their latest metaphors are constants.

The idea that all scientific, psychological, theological, and historical descriptions of intangible realities are metaphors is not my own. It's a perspective that developed during the 1960s and 1970s. Of course, many scientific thinkers—as well as religious believers—object to this idea. Some call it a "popular New Age sentiment." For example, science interpreter Lawrence E. Joseph, who is not unsympathetic to New Age thought, says: "E=mc^2 is not a metaphor. It is a precise symbolic representation of the relationship between energy and matter" (Joseph 1990, 117). But any metaphor can be a precise symbolic representation—and like all metaphors, this one is not the whole story. $E=mc^2$ does not cover everything there is to say about the "relationship between energy and matter."

Despite objections, many theorists in many fields have acknowledged that their descriptions of reality are actually metaphors. As a general principle, we might say that any single description of reality only provides a map of some aspect of reality. But in no case is the map either complete or identical with the reality itself—as many people have pointed out, "the map is not the territory."[1] Any given event or phenomenon has many simultaneously true descriptions, and none of them entirely exhaust the truth.

Let's say, for example, that country A invades country B. We can analyze and describe the event by using political, economic, historical, psychological, chemical, sociological, and moral descriptions. We can understand something about the nature of the event from each of these descriptions. But we needn't decide which one is the "real" cause. That would obstruct a fuller understanding. We might say an economic event—scarcity of fuel—occurred at the time country A invaded country B; or a chemical reaction to medication and a political impulse had a combined impact on the neurosystem of country A's leader when he contemplated ordering the invasion. That doesn't mean the resulting violence was necessarily caused by an economic, chemical, or political reaction. It means no more than that the economic, chemical, and political reactions give us insight into what happened. No absolutely authoritative explanation is necessary or possible.

Like it or not, constructing metaphors and using them to explain a directly experienced insight are part of what happens when ideas—which are intangible—come down from the realm of direct experience to be made into useful information. If these interpretive tools weren't necessary, we'd all be able to grasp our highest ideals and most profound perceptions without controversy. Instead, we are subject to something like a law of conceptual gravity: all descriptions, formulas, theories, and systems are attempts at truth and misrepresentations of truth at the same time.

THE VALUE OF METAPHORIC MEANING

All of the above is by way of recognizing the value of metaphoric meaning. Perhaps it is going a long way round to establish this, but here it is—intangible data that can't be quantified can yield valuable, usable information if we employ a metaphoric system to analyze the data. It doesn't have to be quantum physics, but that's a good example. The system of disciplines used by Yaqui Indian "warriors" to deal with the rich complexity of seen and unseen worlds is a good interpretive tool for understanding the disciplines that have helped women superintendents of schools survive and succeed. It is no romanticization. It is as valid as $E=mc^2$. Both bring a mystery to light and yield fundamental truths that cannot be pressed too hard without blowing up in our faces.

In a historical period where paradigms of explanation are being transformed by new knowledge in all fields of study, it is essential to recognize the value that comes from metaphoric interpretations of intangible data. We need to make use of new insights. Until we once again have a lens reliable enough to help us see the world clearly—and get some consensus on what we are seeing— we ought to look through every device we can that might yield insight and usable information.

CHAPTER 2

GATHERING
INTANGIBLE DATA

THE WOMEN SUPERINTENDENTS
AND THE ASSEMBLY

Narrative data gathered from twelve primary participants—who were superintendents at the time of the study—create the core of this book. The study focuses specifically on women because studies of men in the superintendency have assumed that understanding male behavior is appropriate for the understanding of all behavior (Shakeshaft 1993, 94). But there is suggestive evidence that women generally "see, value, and know" their world differently than men. This difference could, in part, be the reason that few women are superintendents or educational administrators (Belenky, Clinchy, Goldberger, and Tarule 1986; Brunner 1993; Edson 1988; Lather 1991; Ortiz 1982; Sexton 1976; Shakeshaft 1989).

In fact, the underrepresentation of women in the position of superintendent of schools is well known. Depending on the year, between 88 percent and 99 percent of all school superintendents are men despite the prevalence of women in teaching positions (Blount 1993; Glass 1992; Shakeshaft 1989). This figure has varied little over the last century (see Foreword for 1999 figures). Lack of role models, lack of support from networks and mentors, lack of experience in leadership positions in non-governmental institutions, and the greater amount of family demands for women are among the many factors thought to contribute to such under-representation (Campbell 1991; Edson 1988; Lynch, 1990; Marshall 1984; Schmuck 1975; Shakeshaft 1979; Tyack and Hansot 1982;

Whitaker and Lane 1990; Yeakey, Johnston, and Adkison 1986). Therefore, for this study, I purposefully pursued the advice of successful women superintendents with the hope that it would be helpful to other women who are in or are aspiring to educational leadership.

The twelve women chosen for the study were interviewed individually. They did not know each other's names, and it is unlikely that they knew each other at all, given that the study was done nationally. I traveled broadly to gather data from women all over the United States because I was interested in whether my findings would be affected by region or size of district. And while I noted a few minor differences, they were not significant relative to the findings shared in this book.

The lived experiences of the participants served as data for the study. "Data are used differently," as Lather (1991, 150) states, "rather than to support an analysis, they are used demonstrably, performatively." Eisner (1988) supports this particular use of data when he states that "it is more important to understand what people experience than to focus simply on what they do" (x). This focus on the importance of experience in educational research is echoed in the works of Greene (1991), Connelly and Clandenin (1988), Miller (1992), Ayers (1992), and Schubert, (1992). In addition, although there is a current emphasis on the significance of teachers' experiences, very little work has been focused on administrators' experiences; particularly, according to Shakeshaft (1989), there are few individual accounts, biographies, histories, case studies, or ethnographies centered on women administrators (56). This study adds a relevant piece to existing knowledge in educational research by providing individual advice from the lived experiences of exemplary women superintendents who were considered by others to be superior, well liked, successful, and supported in their practice.

While the core of this book is rooted in the narratives of twelve women superintendents, that is not the whole story. Each chapter ends with additional narrative data gathered from a focus group—referred to as the Assembly—of twenty-nine women superintendents and administrators. They met over a period of two years not only to respond, react, and corroborate the data from the primary twelve women, but also to add their own ideas about how meaningful and useful the seven Principles of Power were for their practice as superintendents and administrators.

METHODS AND DESIGN OF THE STUDY

Because the position of superintendent of schools, while powerful, is one with tremendous ethical demands, I chose to search the literature on power and ethics for direction on research methods for this study. In my search I found that feminists point out that debates on power and ethics have been methodologically limited: even those who have challenged orthodox ideas about power and ethics have generally employed traditional scientific and philosophical methods to develop their positions. Of course, conventional scientific methods have proven somewhat useful for describing and explaining the underrepresentation of women in positions of authority. However, the few existing studies of gender differences in political styles did employ different methods; the more ethnographic the research method, the greater the observed style differences between men and women.

Schlozman, Burns, Verba, and Donahue (1995) demonstrated shortcomings of traditional methods. The study's conclusion that women act like men was based on fixed-format questionnaires mailed to members of various groups active in lobbying Washington officials, and there were no opportunities in these questionnaires for female and male respondents to indicate different conceptions of politics and power. In contrast, Kirkpatrick (1974) used more open-ended interviews, and Mansbridge (1986) incorporated participant observation techniques that facilitated greater recognition of distinctive feminine styles in using political power. Schlozman and her collaborators recognized that a feminist conception of power as shared may best be studied through less restrictive qualitative methods than these researchers employed. They exhort "others to use other methods to elaborate upon our results" (Schlozman, Burns, Verba, and Donahue 1995, 289; see also Verba 1990, 569).

Further, such feminists as Sandra Harding (1986, 9) believed that traditional scientific methods serve "regressive social tendencies" and are "culturally coercive" because they take as givens traditional social practices and beliefs. The studies of Lawrence Kohlberg on moral development (1958, 1981) exemplified the inadequacies of traditional methodologies, according to Gilligan (1982). Kohlberg's analytical framework, which employed male idealizations as the standard of justice by which to measure moral development, could not hear or comprehend any alternative moral reasoning—"a different voice," in Gilligan's resonant phrase. Kohlberg's framework could not acknowledge the moral reasoning that derives from different life experiences and values than those of the deductive philosopher or the inductive scientist. Accordingly, Gilligan and other feminists believe that ethics must be understood by letting the moral agent express her own understanding of the requirements of moral action as she experiences them in concrete and personalized circumstances.

In short, a qualitative methodological approach (Guba and Lincoln 1981; Lather 1991; Patton 1980) was necessary for this study to enlarge understanding of the role of women in the superintendency. While the traditional methods of philosophy and science ask whether ideas and the people who hold these ideas conform to preexisting understandings, qualitative research that allows for a less inhibited expression of ideas permits me to question and reconceptualize previous understandings.

SELECTING THE TWELVE WOMEN SUPERINTENDENTS

In order to develop a sample, a modified version of the reputational method from Hunter's (1953) classic community power study of Atlanta was used. To distinguish the most powerful members of the community, Hunter made lists of leaders occupying positions of power in civic organizations, business establishments, and government, as well as persons prominent socially because of their wealth. After compiling lists, he asked long-standing community persons to select and rank people on the lists in a way which identified the most influential leaders.

Hunter's method was modified to fit this study. Working from a national list of women superintendents (approximately 850 women), a panel of experts who know educators was consulted to identify women superintendents whose reputations were regarded as excellent. Contacts included directors of professional organizations, national headhunters, university professors, and people in the private sector.

The final list of superintendents for this study included twelve women from the extreme northeast, northern and central midwest, and extreme southeast portions of the United States. These women had responsibility for districts ranging in size from just under 1,400 to 135,000 students. Five superintendents were responsible for fewer than 4,000 students, two were responsible for between 8,000 to 50,000 students, and five were responsible for 50,000 to 135,000 students.

All of the primary participants were European American[1] and ranged in age from mid-forties to late fifties. Eight had earned doctorates in education, one was working on a dissertation for a doctorate, and three had masters degrees. Six had been in their positions as superintendents for three years or less, and six, for four or more years. Their primary commonalty, other than their position, was that they had reputations for extremely successful performance as superintendent of schools—something confirmed in districts through interview triangulation.

For this study, I interviewed twelve women superintendents and two other people within each school district in order to triangulate data—a total of thirty-six respondents. Superintendents were asked to suggest several people for triangulation interviews whom they believed knew their practice well enough to discuss it. Using availability as a selection device, one administrator and one teacher were interviewed. The main purpose of these interviews was to validate the narratives of the women superintendents and to establish that the women were considered successful superintendents.

The interviews, which were recorded and transcribed, were most often conducted face to face in settings convenient for the participants (often in their offices). (Some triangulation interviews were conducted over the phone.) Interviews were a minimum of an hour in length, and superintendents were interviewed at least twice for a total of fifty-four interviews.

After three introductory questions, the interview approach—for all participants—was non-standardized and guided by cues from the interviewee (Patton 1980; Guba and Lincoln 1981). In addition, I followed guidelines established by Lather (1991) for postpositivist inquiry.

To follow those guidelines, I made certain that the participants were aware of my position in the study—that they understood the biases and past experiences that constructed my point of view. Second interviews with superintendents had two purposes: 1) clarifying the first interviews; and 2) collaborative theory building with the participants. In addition, I followed the advice of the respondents when deciding on the sequencing and timing for triangulation.

DEMOGRAPHICS OF THE ASSEMBLY

The Assembly included twenty-one women superintendents and seven women administrators who were interested in and willing to focus on the seven "Principles of Power" and on the data gathered from the primary twelve women. Over the course of three years (four to five meetings a year), the Assembly met to discuss the Riddle of the Heart, the Seven Principles, the three results of impeccable practice, and my analysis of the narrative data from the twelve women superintendents in the study. The names of some these women—a few wanted to remain anonymous— are in the front of the book. The Assembly discussions were taped and transcribed and later reviewed by all of the participants for their corrections and further input.

The Assembly included one African American and twenty-eight European Americans who lived and worked in Wisconsin and Iowa. Most were superintendents, a few were administrators in other roles. Most

(25) were in districts with fewer than 4,000 students, three were in districts with between 8,000 and 50,000 students, and one was in a district of more than 50,000 students.

They ranged in age from forty to sixty. Most had either an Ed.D. or a Ph.D. (23) and the rest had masters degrees. Nine had been in their positions for three years or less, and fifteen for four or more years.

There were four significant differences between the twelve women superintendents and the Assembly. First, the twelve women were primary participants in a study that followed the rigorous sample development methods discussed in the previous section, while the Assembly was a group of women who expressed an interest in participating.

Second, the interview data of the twelve women were triangulated in other interviews held with at least two other people who knew them. The data gathered from the Assembly was not triangulated. Third, while, as mentioned before, it is unlikely that any of the primary women participants knew each other, I am certain that some of the women in the Assembly knew each other before coming together. Finally, the narrative data gathered during Assembly meetings were from conversation rather than individual interviews. These data are found in all chapters on the principles and all chapters on the three results, in a section labelled "The Assembly."

THE ANALYSIS

As with established methods of qualitative research (Bogdan and Biklen 1992; Glaser and Strauss 1967; Lincoln and Guba 1985; Miles and Huberman 1984; Strauss 1987) narrative data analysis followed the three-part modified constant comparative method developed by Conrad (1982). First, data analysis was done in the field as data were collected and organized in taxonomies.[2] At this level, the analysis helped to create and sharpen additional questions to be used in subsequent interviews. In addition, emerging interpretations were shared with the respondents during the interview process. It was at this juncture in the study, after all of the major themes had surfaced, that I began to see a striking parallel between the findings and the Principles of Power advanced by Carlos Castaneda (1981). More specifically, his Principles of Power for warriors, particularly those governing the Riddle of the Heart, bore an uncanny parallel to the emerging themes in the data. At that time, I decided to use the principles as taxonomies to organize the data. In order to test the appropriateness of the principles as organizing taxonomies, I contacted three of the women in the study. All three were enthusiastic about the relationship between Castaneda's principles and their methods for success as superintendents. They were encouraged when they saw that their experiences could be communicated to others in a way—through metaphor—that removed the stigma that sometimes accompanies gender-specific advice. The analysis using Castaneda's Principles of Power as a vehicle for communicating the findings continued.

Another layer of analysis occurred during the discussions of the Assembly. In these discussions, my analyses of the twelve women superintendents' narratives were examined and enhanced. Further, analysis of the Assembly's narrative data was a part of the process. Members of the Assembly analyzed their own transcripts, editing and clarifying to make meanings clearer. In addition, they "talked back" to my interpretations of what they said. The process was truly a collaborative one.

Finally, data analysis occurred during the writing process so that what was seen and heard could be written as clearly as possible for the reader (Lincoln and Guba 1985).

CHAPTER 3

EMBODYING INTANGIBLE DATA

THE WOMEN AS WARRIORS

Carlos Castaneda was an anthropologist whose studies revolved around a Yaqui Indian from northern Mexico, Don Juan Matus. According to Castaneda in *The Eagle's Gift* (1981, 1), Don Juan was a practitioner "of ancient knowledge, which in our time is commonly known as . . . psychological science, but which in fact is a tradition of extremely self-disciplined practitioners and extremely sophisticated praxes." While studying, Castaneda became an apprentice to Don Juan, and Castaneda's books share his new knowledge with readers.

A COMPLEX METAPHOR

In *The Power of Silence: Further Lessons of Don Juan*, Castaneda (1987) relates Don Juan's system for teaching warriors.[1] It may hit you wrong, this combining of women superintendents and the term *warrior*. But then, you may also find the term *women superintendents* is an oxymoron. In other words, both terms—*warrior* and *superintendent*—have been considered masculine. So much so that it is difficult to see in one's mind's eye anything but a man when the terms are used. This issue presents a complex problem to readers.

The complexity of visualizing a woman when the term *superintendent* is used, is precisely why a particular metaphor (Carlos Castaneda's) of the "warrior" is so useful when describing the work of women superintendents. It is Castaneda's metaphoric descriptions of the Principles of Power practiced by warriors that bring to life the deeper, more instructive messages from women superintendents as they talk about their work and personal lives. Why? Because Castaneda's stories of the Yaqui Indians and their sacred training for their spiritual leaders—their warriors—combine the masculine and feminine forces found in all of life. In fact, the majority of Castaneda's books include as many women as men in spiritual warrior training.

For most Americans, the natural combination of masculine and feminine forces within the same body or structure is a foreign notion. Instead, we tend to polarize the two forces, with specific descriptions of what is feminine and what is masculine. In Castaneda's work, however, the interaction and interdependence of the two forces are intricately woven into the fabric of the Seven Principles of Power. In such a context, the words *women* and *superintendent* are no longer mutually exclusive. The term *warrior* embodies both feminine and masculine energies.

Castaneda's books are not the only place to find a larger, full-bodied, use of the term *warrior*. As Hillman (1994) relates, "In our most elevated works of thought—Hindu and Platonic philosophy—a warrior class is imagined as necessary to the well-being of humankind. This class finds its counter part within human nature, in the heart, as virtues of courage, nobility, honor, loyalty, steadfastness of principle, comradely love, so that war is given location not only in a class of persons but in a level human personality organically necessary to the justice of the whole" (72). The warrior of the heart is an archetype that has space for both genders.

Warriors are most often thought to have weapons of some type. What, then, are the basic "weapons" of the warrior of the heart. According to Welwood (1994, 99), the weapons are: awareness, courage, and gentleness. He states that these weapons "cut through our habitual tendencies to fight or flee when we come up against painful or difficult situations. In this way, they allow us to convert whatever challenges we are facing into stepping stones in our development" (99).

Certainly, the women superintendents in the study faced challenges with courage. They faced issues of overt and covert gender bias as they moved into the masculinized world of educational administration. They understood that every obstacle or challenge they faced contained implicit questions which determined new directions in their lives. As Angeles Arrien (1994) suggests, "It is important to remember that when challenges present themselves, it is the warrior's way to embrace them with full-bodied presence rather than to constrict in fear" (111). They did not give in to hopelessness. Rather they embraced challenge and appreciated themselves as women. Using their experiences as stepping stones, they developed the characteristics of warriors. Eventually, they were not afraid of who they were.

Rick Fields (1994) quotes Chogyam Trungpa who said, "The key to warriorship is not being afraid of who you are. Ultimately, that is the definition of bravery: not being afraid of yourself." Fields continues, "Such bravery involves discipline and training, of course, but it also involves being kind and vulnerable, both to ourselves and others" (xvi).

Not being afraid of self meant that the women superintendents cherished and celebrated their own individual being and femaleness. They seemed to believe, as many indigenous societies, that they possessed "original medicine," a power that resides within each person that is not duplicated anywhere else on the planet (Arrien 1993, 21). They were proud to be women and determined to be warriors. And while they also struggled with common human limitations, Mirtha Vega's "The Warrioress Creed," describes them as well as anything I have found.

> A Warrioress . . .
> is honorable;
> has strength, determination, and perseverance;
> is magical and optimistic;
> is wise and powerful;
> revels in silence;
> can appreciate both inner and outer beauty;
> is dedicated to the sacredness of her life;
> loves to live fully;
> is unwavering in her quest for the infinite;
> is respectful;
> can commit to those she deems worthy;
> can let go of what is no longer useful, or necessary;
> is compassionate;
> possesses the will to walk away from illusion;
> is willing to trust and surrender when appropriate;
> has extraordinary vision and clarity;
> faces her fears head-on;
> believes.
>
> (Vega 1994, 89)

The archetype of the warrior works as an embodiment of the intangible data that I gathered when working with the women superintendents in the study. It represents the full nature and energy of the women in ways that cannot be expressed with words. After all, "[t]his archetypal warrior energy is one of the most powerful forces of the human psyche. . . . [W]hen it is properly honored, honed, and disciplined, when we know how to work with it, the warrior within can be the source of tremendous good. Without a well-developed warrior spirit, it is difficult to accomplish anything worthwhile" (Fields 1994, xv).

Expressing things that cannot be expressed with words is complex. Metaphor facilitates that expression and, still, does not completely accomplish it. That the complete expression is not accomplished through metaphor must be remembered as this book is read. As Thomas Pynchon (1966) reminds us, "Metaphor is a thrust at truth and a lie" (129). This paradox is yet another layer of complexity.

EVEN FURTHER COMPLEXITY

On one hand, this book is simple in ways. To be sure, the structure is simple. The first part is introductory, the second is substance, and third is conclusion. On the other hand, this book is complex in the ways listed previously. In fact, it has yet another layer of complexity. That final layer is in the ultimate grasping of the meaning of the book. Let me explain.

First, it is not that the concepts are difficult. In fact, many of them are familiar. Further, the writing is straightforward and plain. Instead, the final and perhaps most important complexity is related to the interconnectedness of the Riddle of the Heart, the Seven Principles of Power, and the three results of impeccable practice. Or more to the point, the complexity is in the comprehension of Carlos Castaneda's (1981) metaphoric system of the Seven Principles of Power governing the Riddle of the Heart and seeing the system's application to the lives of women superintendents.

The fact that language is linear becomes problematic when writing about things that are intangible, and although metaphor is tremendously helpful when conveying intangible ideas, it is clear that communication about such things is never complete.

If I could, I would communicate the entire book to the reader in the span of one moment. I would create a nonlinear experience of some kind so that the interconnections would be inherently understood. Nothing would stand alone in chapters or in separate ideas. And while Carlos Castaneda—whose work I use as metaphor—had the same limitations of language as I do, his retelling of his experiences with Don Juan pulls the reader into the events of the story. If the reader can suspend disbelief, something of the story-event causes a change of mind in the reader. Perhaps one day I will tell the stories about women superintendents in ways that communicate their meanings in a similar fashion.

For the purposes of this book, however, research is the foundation of the writing, and research has prescriptive methods for coming into text. And while I have pushed the limits of traditional research by using Carlos Castaneda's Principles of Power as metaphor to express intangible data, I still cling to the traditional modes of logical, linear, disciplined thought for transferring ideas to the reader. Therein lies the complexity of the book.

PART TWO

METAPHOR

ARTICULATING INTANGIBLES

Metaphors are the primary human tool for grasping the intangible

—R. M. Olderman, *Alien Information*

In order to write a clear translation from the data gathered in interviews, I used Castaneda's (1981) metaphors of the warrior, the Warrior's Path, and mastery of the Riddle of the Heart (see Figure 1) to organize the data. This metaphor helped me flesh out the meanings of the more elusive and intangible qualities of women in the superintendency. The use of metaphor is particularly appropriate in this connection because "[t]he essence of metaphor is understanding and experiencing one kind of thing in terms of another" (Lakoff and Johnson 1980, 5). Further, because "[t]hrough transfer of *meaning*, metaphors broaden perspectives, enhance understanding and provide insight . . ." (Bredeson 1988, 293), metaphors are a linguistic device of great value when describing the position of superintendent to women who have never been in the position or are wanting to know what it "takes" for a woman to be successful in the role of superintendent.

This section begins with a chapter that describes fully the Riddle of the Heart. Following that are seven chapters, each in turn devoted to one Principle of Power and the narratives of the women superintendents,

which reveal how they have approached the demands of the superintendency. It is through the interaction of Castaneda's principles and the
practices of the women in the study that the articulation of practice
becomes deeply meaningful and understandable for the reader. The principles both illuminate and are, in turn, supported by the narrative data
from the interviews with women superintendents. All twelve women are
represented numerous times in the text.

THE WARRIOR'S PATH

GOAL:

TO MASTER THE RIDDLE OF THE HEART

KEY TO THE RIDDLE:

CARING IN RELATIONSHIPS

Caring must be acted out through
Impeccable Practice of

SEVEN PRINCIPLES OF POWER:

1. Knowing the Battleground
2. Discarding the Unnecessary
3. Choosing Battles
4. Taking Risks
5. Seeking Retreat
6. Compressing Time
7. Exercising Power

RESULTS IN

Evidence of Mastery of

RIDDLE OF THE HEART:

1. Laughing at Self
2. Patience Without Fretting
3. Improvisation

FIGURE 1.

CHAPTER 4

THE WARRIOR'S PATH

THE RIDDLE OF THE HEART AND
THE SEVEN PRINCIPLES OF POWER

Carlos Castaneda (1981) relates that according to don Juan's system for teaching warriors, apprentices are schooled toward three areas of expertise; the mastery of awareness, the mastery of intent, and the art of stalking.[1] He states that

> [t]hese three areas of expertise are the three riddles [warriors] encounter in their search for knowledge. The mastery of awareness is the riddle of the mind; . . . The mastery of intent is the riddle of the spirit, or the paradox of the abstract. . . . The art of stalking is the riddle of the heart; it is the puzzlement [warriors] feel upon becoming aware of two things: first, that the world appears to us to be unalterably objective and factual because of peculiarities of our awareness and perception; [and] second, that if different peculiarities of perception come into play, the very things about the world that seem so unalterably objective and factual change. (14–15)

It is the "Riddle of the Heart" that resonates with the perspectives of the successful women superintendents in the study.

Warriors who wish to solve the Riddle of the Heart (see Figure 1, p. 25) must first find the key to the Riddle and, second, must master the Riddle. In order to master it, warriors must move down the Warrior's Path by impeccably practicing the Seven Principles of Power. Once they are impeccably practiced, mastery of the Riddle of the Heart is possible. Such mastery results in three tangible things: the ability to laugh at self; the ability to be patient without fretting; and the ability to improvise. Mastery of the Riddle of the Heart also results in an intangible ability described in the next paragraph.

The metaphor of mastering the Riddle of the Heart can be used to describe the successful practice of the women superintendents in the study. Using the metaphor, it could be said that the women superintendents in the study took the Warrior's Path after uncovering the key to the Riddle—caring in relationships (see Figure 1). They then used the Seven Principles of Power to gain mastery of the Riddle. Mastery meant that they gained the three tangible abilities, and the intangible ability to simultaneously comprehend and make use of two different perceptions of the world and/or know how to exist within a shifting system of perceptions while a new world view slowly replaces an old one.

The women in the study looked past what the world has normally perceived to be factual—that only authoritarian structures make superintendents succeed, and that only men can be superintendents. They moved their own perceptions into play so that the "very things about the world that seem so unalterably objective and factual [could actually] change."

Their perceptions of the superintendency included not only putting women in the role, but also included a "feminine" sense of ethics, what Noddings (1984) refers to as an "ethic of care." This deep sense of caring was evidence of their shifted system of perceptions. It was the evidence that they had found the warrior's key to the Riddle of the Heart.

Through their feminine practice, the nature of the superintendency changed into a job of heartfelt caring. They understood the warrior's caring nature. As Fields (1994) said, "Like the thorn on the rose, the warrior is pledged to protect whatever is lovely, vulnerable, and truly precious. This may include the warrior's own life, but it does not stop with self-interest. The warrior's care and protection extends outward in an ever-widening circle, from family, tribe, king, nation, and not to earth herself" (xv).

The literature in educational administration supports such a change. To be sure, when "we look clear-eyed" at the position of the superintendent of schools, "we see it wracked" with "psychic pain of all sorts" (Noddings 1984, 1). The sources of this pain are numerous (Arnez 1981; Blumberg 1985; Griffiths 1966; Leithwood 1995; Moore-Johnson 1996; Tyack and Hansot 1982), but perhaps the most obvious is the external pressure from conflicting constituencies and interest groups (Crowson 1992; Lutz and Mertz 1992). Superintendents may desire to respond and act appropriately, carefully, and with care, but as Beck (1994) identifies:

[C]onscientious school officers are likely to find themselves
rushing from one crisis to another, taking action to quell the
more obvious or serious problems before moving on to other
issues. Clearly, what is needed is an organizing perspective, an
understanding of education and leadership, which can assist
leaders in sifting through and prioritizing demands and in
making wise decisions regarding their actions and responses.
(58)

Beck proposes that an ethic of caring could "provide a solid foundation for such a perspective." She also offers a caring ecological
model of schooling which responds to challenges she believes to be
pivotal in discussions of educators' tasks (58). The challenges she identifies are: "1) administering schools in ways that result in improved
performances—of students and teachers; 2) addressing a host of social
problems within and through schools; and 3) rethinking organizational
structures so that schools will be better able to meet the preceding
challenges" (58).

The reason I am interested in this particular approach to practice in
the superintendency is because superintendents not only experience "pain"
while in their positions, but are also, like Noddings and Beck, concerned
about the pain in the world.

The women superintendents in the study suggest that the current
structure of governance in schools—one of authority or control, endorsed
by our culture and expected of superintendents does not support their
desire to substantively address some of the widespread pain in our environment. They found a new beginning point from which to address this
widespread pain.

Such a beginning point is also suggested by Noddings (1984) when
she states that relation is ontologically basic, which means that she recognizes human encounter and affective response as a basic fact of human
existence.

This suggests that the ethic to be developed is one of reciprocity, but our view of reciprocity will be different from that
of "contract" theorists such as Plato and John Rawls. . . . The
focus of our attention will be upon how to meet the other
morally. Ethical caring, the relation in which we do meet the
other morally, . . . [arises] out of natural caring—that relation
in which we respond as one-caring out of love or natural
inclination. The relation of natural caring [is] identified as the
human condition that we, consciously or unconsciously, perceive as "good." (4–5)

The need to "meet the other morally," reflects the experiences of the women superintendents in the study. As public school superintendents, the twelve women worked to relate to others in a way informed by their own senses of morality. I came to understand that like Noddings (1984), they believed that relation is "ontologically basic" and caring relation is "ethically basic" (3). They were dissatisfied with certain dominant but limited views such as: superintendents and their governance structures control others; "ethics" are principles of justice; and moral practice means the achievement of objectivity and detachment rather than the ability to engage responsively and with care (Gilligan 1982, xix). They wished for a way to talk and think about these concepts that resonated with their predispositions toward and perceptions of the role of superintendent.

I came to understand that the motivation behind the desire of the women in the study to talk and think about these concepts in new ways was their love of and care for children. Their perceptions of practice were rooted in and, indeed, driven by their love and care for children. This perception of practice as "care" drove a wedge of frustration between their own culturally created views of the position of superintendent and their own understandings of the role. In an unschooled, instinctual way they battled against the narrow conception of ethics as a hierarchy of justice. Unaware and in unarticulated parallel action, they advanced what Carol Gilligan (1982) initiated—the feminist attack on the narrow conceptions of the ethics of justice that preoccupy contemporary political philosophy.

According to Gilligan, moral philosophers have assumed that the ethics of justice requires acting on the basis of some formal and abstract principles that prioritize competing rights. Gilligan suggests that such conceptions of ethics reflect a masculine morality that emphasizes the formal rules of (boys') games, rather than a feminine morality that emphasizes the give and take and contexts of human relationships.[2] Noddings (1984, 1992), Tronto (1994), and others have asserted that theories of ethics cannot be completely specified through abstract principles, but must also encompass "an ethic of care."

For example, Nel Noddings (1984) moves ethics, the philosophical study of morality, from a concentration on the masculinized hierarchical moral reasoning of principles to the feminized moral responsiveness of human caring and the memory of caring and being cared for (1). She argues that ethics approached through law and principles is, in the classical sense, the approach of the detached one, of the father, not of the mother (2). The approach of the mother is feminine in that it is "rooted in receptivity, relatedness, and responsiveness," but

[t]his does not imply that all women will accept it or that men will reject it; indeed, there is no reason why men should not embrace it. . . . It does not imply either that logic is to be discarded or that logic is alien to women. It represents an alternative to present views, one that begins with the moral attitude or longing for goodness and not with moral reasoning. (2)

Women, Noddings asserts, ask for more information when they are confronted with a hypothetical moral dilemma. They want to talk to people so they can see their eyes and facial expressions and to somehow experience what they are feeling. Noddings continues,

Moral decisions are, after all, made in real situations; they are qualitatively different from the solution of geometry problems. Women can and do give reasons for their acts, but the reasons often point to feelings, needs, impressions, and sense of personal ideal rather than to universal principles and their application. . . . [A]s a result of this "odd" approach women have often been judged inferior to men in the moral domain. (2–3)

In the same vein, Gilligan (1982) pointed out the importance for women of a morality defined as care for and sensitivity to others when she discussed the work of several well-known theorists in psychology and education—Freud, Piaget, and Kohlberg. For example, she reminded her readers that Kohlberg's (1958) theory of six stages of moral development is derived from his empirical work based on a study of eighty-four boys whose development he followed for more than twenty years. Girls simply "did not exist" in the study, which was generalized across gender, race, sexual preference, and class (Gilligan, 18). And, "[a]lthough Kohlberg claims universality for his stage sequence, those groups not included in his original sample rarely reach his higher stages" (Edwards 1975; Holstein 1976; Simpson 1974 cited in Gilligan 1982, 18).

Women, in fact, when measured by Kohlberg's scale appear to be deficient in moral development because their

judgments seem to exemplify the third stage of his six-stage sequence. At this stage morality is conceived in interpersonal terms and goodness is equated with helping and pleasing others. This conception of goodness is considered by Kohlberg and Kramer (1969) to be functional in the lives of mature women insofar as their lives take place in the home. Kohlberg and Kramer imply that only if women enter the traditional arena of male activity will they recognize the inadequacy of

this moral perspective and progress like men toward higher
stages where relationships are subordinated to rules (stage
four) and rules to universal principles of justice (stages five and
six). (Gilligan 1982, 18)

It is this conception of goodness characteristic of Kohlberg and Kramer's
third stage of moral development, however, that reflects an ethic of care.
Feminists have also noted that studies of justice address how fairly
justice is distributed among a nation's citizens (Kuenne 1993) or various
political subcommunities (Mier 1993; Mladenka 1980), and have ignored
the distribution of justice in the family and other nongovernmental social
units. Yet some of the greatest injustices occur within these latter institutions (Kozol 1991). According to Susan Okin (1989), the failure to recognize that "the personal is the political" has been a grave defect of justice
theories. Injustices that occur in our most personal social units, such as
families and schools, contribute to larger social injustices because families,
schools, and other face-to-face institutions are the training grounds for
citizens. Such feminists as Kay Boals (1975) and Paula Baker (1984) thus
argued that politics is a much more inclusive activity than the actions
taken (or not taken) by governmental authorities or through governmental institutions. Boals and Baker have inferred that justice requires a
fair distribution of goods among members of voluntary associations as
well as within governmental jurisdictions.

Ethical practices centered on fair distribution of goods are important
in schools. Again, it is the practice of an ethic of care that forces people
to pay attention to helping others—especially students—receive their fair
share of resources and opportunity in school settings. This is a worthy
goal for those in the superintendency. It is truly a goal of the heart.

It is this goal that the women in the study perceived to be the most
important work of superintendents. And, it is this "peculiar" or unusual
perception of the superintendency that changes the position when these
women occupy it. Thus, one of the things in the world—the superintendency—that seems so unalterable can change. Women can be superintendents, and superintendents can practice in a caring way, prioritizing
relationships and children. The act of caring, an ethic of care, is the key
to the Riddle of the Heart.

TWELVE WOMEN SUPERINTENDENTS AND CARING

The larger goal of caring was a significant part of the rhetoric and practice of the women in the study. This goal found expression in their practice

and rhetoric in two primary areas: 1) relationships in general; and, most important, 2) the well-being, both academically and generally, of the children in their districts.

The topic of relationships was articulated in a variety of ways. One superintendent referred to caring throughout her interview particularly in regard to relationships. For example, when asked how she accomplished things, she replied,

> Well, I think that what you do is you are able to admire the human resources of your staff and build personal relationships with highly talented people who want to grow, and who want to be their very best.

She continued by focusing on the importance of people around her:

> I think the third necessary component is the network, and that probably builds personal contact with people with whom you share ideas, information, and resources.

In reference to herself when asked about her leadership style, she said,

> About my own personal style, I know that I'm a very caring person. . . . I don't ever try to deny my femininity in my leadership role.

Another superintendent talked about how she made certain that people were "taken care of" by making certain that they felt success in their work in the district. Even when decisions were made collaboratively, if somehow the decision brought "grief," she would "take" the grief. Conversely, she believed that any credit that was positive should go to the group.

> No matter which way the decision goes, and who had the greatest influence on making it, if anything is wrong, I will take all the grief for it, you know. I will not take the good things for it because that goes to the people who have input. I firmly believe that if I absorb failure, then everybody else feels success.

Another woman discussed how she had at one time executed a principled practice that she reported "was politically correct"—something that felt foreign to her—when making decisions that she felt were, in principle, "right" for others. She soon discovered a discomfort with this practice because she sensed that she was manipulating people. She changed her practice for the sake of honesty and "goodness" in her relationships with people.

> I pretty soon found out that people were doing what I was manipulating them into doing. And I, of course, believed that I was manipulating them into doing the right thing. But as I reflect today I believe that I was just being politically correct [something generally thought to be ethical]. I began to feel very dishonest. There are times when I could use that same skill and feel justified because it is generally thought to be ethical, but I don't. Instead, I definitely try to listen to input from people.

Another superintendent talked about the "caring" that she believed others expected of her because she was a woman, something she felt would not be expected of men in the position.

> And I think that you would find that in this position, for example, board members will ask a female superintendent to do things she would never even consider asking a male superintendent to do. And by that I mean it's the expectation that a female will know about the details, is responsible for the caring of fifteen thousand employees. Whereas the expectation is that a man shouldn't or isn't expected to do all the "nits and grits" plus all of the big decision making.

The second strong component of the narratives in regard to caring was the intense focus these women placed on the children literally "in their care" in their districts. I learned that the lives of children were of utmost importance to these women. Certainly, the nurturing of children has been an unquestioned part of what is most often the "feminine" domain. It was clear that the women superintendents in the study had prioritized relationships and children while in the position of superintendent of schools. For the full discussion of the women and their caring ethic toward children, see chapter 7.

WHAT OTHER PEOPLE SAID ABOUT THE CARING ATTITUDES OF THE TWELVE WOMEN

It was important to me to fully understand the practices of the women in the study, so I spent a great deal of time in interviews with people who knew them. In several cases, I interviewed more than two people who knew the women. In some cases (the larger districts), I interviewed more than fifty people. It was in the triangulation interviews that I came to understand the breadth and depth of the caring practices of the women superintendents.

I did not ask people direct questions, during triangulation interviews, about the caring practices of the woman superintendents, but the
narrative data provided abundant evidence. References to the women's
focus on relationships were frequent and varied. One assistant superintendent noted that her superintendent always made certain that everyone
got public credit for her/his input. The superintendent's caring, attentive
attitude was also evident in the way the assistant superintendent talked
about the faith the superintendent had in everyone. She said,

> With Doctor [Name], it's like everything is laid out in the
> open, and you have the responsibility to share what you have
> with others and make certain that communication flows
> constantly through the organization. No information is with-
> held from us. Then when decisions are made, she will make
> certain that everyone knows who was involved in the decision
> made. . . . She has a lot of faith in the opinions and beliefs of
> the group—of everyone.

Many comments were made in triangulation interviews about the way
women superintendents differ from men in the same position. Most felt
that the difference centered on the "way women are"—that is, women are
"naturally" more concerned about relationships and do the "nice" things
that make people "feel good." Women who did not do these things were
viewed as "cold" and somehow less female. A male assistant superintendent made a statement directly related to the difference he saw in the practice of women superintendents and that of men superintendents.

> I think that the entire perspective of women is different in
> how they interact with others. I think they are more nurturing
> by nature. . . . I just feel that they look at things differently
> than men often times—that there are things that they see and
> feel and enunciate that often are missed by men.

When talking about another superintendent, one man referred to the
collaborative process as one that was not only a process for decision
making, but also a process that allowed for taking care of the feelings of
people who were working together.

> I see a lot of qualities of collaboration [in decision making]
> that are tied in with people's feelings in addition to the tasks
> that need to be accomplished.

At least one superintendent was extremely careful of the feelings of
others even when she was angry. A female high school principal reported
the following:

Sometimes I have heard people say that Doctor [Name] just shouldn't try to be so nice to everybody. So they're sort of saying that at times she should just tell somebody off. Well, that really is not her style. Even when she is angriest, whether it's a board member or a businessman, I have not seen her literally tell anyone off. I mean she will be assertive and say what she wants to say but she never makes it a personal attack.

The evidence that these women "care for" people was best reflected in the following statement from a male elementary principal:

I think that [Name] is a very open, friendly person. I think she is very approachable and she has a nice way of interacting with people so they feel comfortable initially at the beginning of a meeting. Not just jumping into it, and, you know, she moves ahead to make sure people are comfortable, and she takes the time to know people and what's happening there, in their life. It's surprising how attentive to that sort of thing she is. Not that she delves into it too much, but she always pays attention to people when something is going on in their life. They maybe need a little extra time, or they need a little bit of support. She's very good about that.

When respondents talked about their superintendents' attention to children, they usually referred to the great commitment that their superintendents had to the scholarship of the students in their districts. One male assistant superintendent expressed the opinion of many when he stated:

She talks about children, decisions made in light of children and the relationship to learning and the setting and the teachers. Her greatest focus is on children learning. I hear that a lot, all of the time.

WOMEN SUPERINTENDENTS AND THE PRINCIPLES OF POWER

From the study, I came to understand that the presence of women in the superintendency has tremendous potential to change the specific common perceptions that have, in the past, disallowed women the position. In fact, their caring practice and heartfelt perceptions are suggestive changes for the way all people—men and women—can perform while in the position of superintendent.

It was their love of children that caused them to do their work in the superintendency in the first place. They all professed a deep love of children, and a desire to do everything they could to better the lives and learning of students under their care. They understood the "Riddle of the Heart" by working within the principles of power that govern the riddle.

INTRODUCING THE SEVEN PRINCIPLES OF POWER

In *The Eagle's Gift*, Castaneda (1981) described the Principles of Power governing the Riddle of the Heart as "a set of procedures and attitudes that [one uses] to get the best out of any conceivable situation" (4). Both the principles and their intended goal of solving the Riddle of the Heart provide an appropriate metaphoric framework for describing the "procedures and attitudes" that the women in the study used to get the best out of their situations as superintendents. Each of the principles is related and interconnected with all of the others, so it is difficult to see where one principle ends and another begins. Apparently it is important to practice them all in unison, rather than in any defined sequence. Because of the interconnectedness of the principles, strict categorization of the narrative data is somewhat arbitrary—there are times when the narrative embodies more than one principle. (See Figure 1) I have left it to the reader to draw the cross-principle connections.

Regardless of its imprecise and incomplete quality, the metaphoric framework employing the Principles of Power is compelling because it supplies a tool for expressing a tradition of rigorous practice that exemplifies, dignifies, and substantiates a previously overlooked body of knowledge or way of knowing. Just such a body of knowledge has been generated through the voices and lives of women superintendents in the study. The rest of the chapters in this section develop each individual principle and its connection to particular procedures and attitudes lived out by the women in the study.

CHAPTER 5

PRINCIPLE ONE

KNOWING THE BATTLEGROUND

The first principle of [power] is that warriors choose their battleground. . . . . A warrior never goes into battle without knowing what the surroundings are.

—Carlos Castaneda, *The Eagle's Gift*

Castaneda, when talking about the First Principle, warns readers about the foolishness of having inflated ideas about themselves. It is inflated senses of self that cause people to be insensitive to their surroundings and walk into traps. So, the first principle focuses on a warrior's sensitivity to her surroundings.

Like this first principle, most of the mainstream literature on leadership strongly advises leaders to know their surroundings, to know the culture (Bolman and Deal 1991). For women, however, this principle has additional implications. Because of the gender-related struggles women face in the superintendency, the metaphor of the "warrior in battle" is appropriate for describing women seeking success.

Most of the women in the study stated that part of "knowing their surroundings" was *their awareness of what was expected of them.* They discussed the importance of knowing that expectations included not only those typical for superintendents, but additional ones related to being a woman in a position most often filled by a man. They clearly knew that their success depended on meeting these gender-specific expectations. For example, a woman from a large district stated:

> I think when you put a female in a position that has been predominately held by men, the expectation in the business community is to see a man. And when they see a woman, their expectation is that she is to do everything the female of the culture has always done—that is to pay attention to detail, to be caring, to do everything you would expect a female to do.

This woman knew her surroundings. And her knowledge created her understanding that she was required to do more as a superintendent than was usually expected. It became clear that this type of knowledge is essential for women superintendents because there are unusual dangers and pitfalls for women when they don't know their surroundings as well as they should.

Several of the women in the study talked about how they learned the First Principle the "hard way." One woman shared this story:

> Well, you know, when you walk into a system where it was an "old boy" system, and people were promoted because they were part of the group, and you are not part of that system— and then you are asked to cut your senior staff by fifteen percent. You have to cut not knowing anybody. I mean, I didn't know who was a friend of a friend of a friend. I was left with a lot of negative feelings against me. So, I probably should have insisted on bringing more people in with me in order to have a cadre of supporters. I think we [as women] need that initially. You have to have people around you that support you just to talk with.

Because of her experiences, this woman was acutely aware that women in the superintendency have to understand that they are outsiders to the "male system." A partial solution, she believed, was to bring your own "surroundings" or system with you.

The superintendents in the study said that to be successful they had to address and balance both role-related and gender-related expectations—expectations that often resulted in contradictory experiences of power and subjection. I came to understand that contradictions are part of the battleground for women superintendents, and their knowledge of and preparation for these contradictory experiences determine whether they succeed in the role.

For example, for the women in the study, expectations or negative gender stereotypes associated with being a woman conflicted with meeting the expectations for being a successful superintendent. Consider the cultural stereotype that women are less able to work with money or in business than men. Role expectations for successful superintendents include financial and business expertise. These two expectations, one for women as women and the other for women as superintendents, are clearly opposed. One superintendent addressed this tension.

> I think that a large group of them [board of education members] wanted an education system that would attract a lot of people and businesses to this community. They believed that with excellent educational system businesses would be very willing to locate here because they wouldn't have trouble moving their families. They wanted to be able to rave about their test scores, you know, and say that we have the jewel of the state's educational system. But they did not want to pay the in order to do that. And part of that price was to be able to clean up what was going on within the system where money was flowing out of the system into the pockets of the business people and out of the classrooms.
>
> So I did that [stopped the flow of money into the hands of powerful business when she worked to save the district money] and I lost the business community's support. And it makes no difference what you do [managing myriad things on very few dollars] they [business connections] will still decide they can't afford you. They begin to say that, number one, you don't have financial and business expertise. It makes no difference that you can sit down and put the facts on the table.
>
> First of all, most don't believe a woman's going to have business expertise—so that's very easy to sell. You do not expect a woman to really be smart in business. You do expect her to be a good teacher, a good little teacher. And no one's ever faulted me on any educational decision that's made. They say, "Well she knows what she's doing in education. She's really brilliant in education, but she really doesn't understand business."

As is apparent in the quote above, some of the discussion in this chapter reflects the complexity and relationship between role-related and gender-related expectations of the women. While in the role of superintendent of schools, the women in the study did not go through a hierarchical form of reasoning to balance or blend these two coexisting sets of expectations. At times one set took precedence over the other set; at times the two sets were given equal attention.

In addition to the overarching "knowledge of their surroundings"—understanding role-related and gender-related expectations of the position—the women in the study knew the details of those expectations. They told me how careful they were in the way they dressed, the importance of a doctorate degree, their willingness to work eighty-hour weeks, their connections to the power networks in the community, and the necessity of a male advocate when applying for a position.

Knowing about demands and having the skills to respond to them was believed to be basic for survival in the battleground of the superintendency but didn't alone ensure success for women. These skills are reflected in the literature on women in positions of power (see for example: Cantor and Bernay 1992; Dunlap and Schmuck 1995; Brunner 1993, 1999; Edson 1988; Epstein 1970; Faludi 1991; Frieze, Parsons, Johnson, Ruble, and Zellman 1978; Hennig and Jardim 1977; Kanter 1977; Vanello and Siemienska 1990).

And while there are gender-specific aspects of each of these skills and demands, perhaps the single most important thing that the women in the study had to know in order to survive the battleground was how to communicate.

At first glance, this finding is not surprising. Without a doubt, almost any book you pick up on leadership emphasizes that leaders must have strong communication skills. What is surprising, however, is that the things that the women needed to know about communication varied in significant ways from what is suggested by the general literature on the superintendency. And the reason for this difference is plain and simple: the women superintendents in the study had to know their surroundings well enough to survive and succeed in a world where communication was shaped and defined by men.

What exactly did this difference mean for the women? First, it meant that learning to communicate effectively required a warrior's skills. It meant that they had to understand the paradoxical nature of their surroundings and remember that: *Women superintendents need to develop the ability to remain "feminine" in the ways they communicate and at the same time be heard in the masculinized culture.* In the struggle to achieve this, the women in the study experienced four specific challenges to successful communication. I have labelled these challenges as: 1) Being silenced by the term *power*; 2) Overt silencing; 3) Listening as different than silence; and 4) Ways of communicating to be heard.

SILENCED BY THE TERM *POWER*

Most of the superintendents in the study had difficulty communicating with me about power. They didn't want to be associated with the concept of power as the dominant culture defines it. They were, in fact, silenced by the topic. In various ways, they related to me that while in their superintendency surroundings, they could not communicate in any way that they had power in the traditional sense if they wanted to be accepted and supported in the role. The full discussion of this phenomenon can be found in chapter 11.

OVERT SILENCING

While numerous feminist scholars have written about "silence" (for example, see Belenky, Clinchy, Goldberger, Tarule 1986; Bernard 1973; Collins 1991; Gilligan 1982; Miller 1976; Olsen 1978; Rich 1979; Tannen 1990), few[1] have focused on the silence of women in powerful masculinized positions such as the superintendency. And because women superintendents are known to speak, one might believe that the power inherent in such a position overrides much of the disallowing of voice or the "unnatural silence" (Olsen 1978) that constrains most women. I found the opposite. The superintendents in my study experienced unnatural silencing in a variety of ways.

One superintendent talked about body language—school board members who turned away when she spoke.

> Sometimes I experience body language when I'm speaking, very negative body language, particularly when I'm speaking to the board as a group, as a whole. And it's eye rolling, sighs, shoulder sagging, closed, arms come folded, talking while I'm talking. It talks pretty loud.

Another woman reported that, at times, board members just didn't listen while she was presenting information—something she had not seen happen to men in her position.

> The biggest thing though is they don't really want to listen to me. They've already decided what the situation is long before I've even begun to speak.

Others talked about meetings with their male colleagues, who dominated, interrupted, talked about topics either uninteresting or inappropriate for women, and, in general, left them out of conversations.

> If I'm talking to a group of males I find that they are more apt to do more talking than a group of women. Stereotypically we picture that women do more talking than men, and I've not found that to be true. I find that men like to hear themselves talk. They talk more. They talk louder. I'm not sure they're always listening. It's a learning process. They just talk. But they're very boisterous, they tend to butt in, they're louder.

> Women are always said to be the talkers, and I don't find
> that. I find other women and me in the group sitting back
> more not being willing to speak out because we seem to be
> dismissed. I mean we kind of get like a headshake, and then
> they go on to the next male.

This superintendent is clearly talking about interruptions that subordinate her to the men in a group. The men she refers to are not interrupting in the way referred to as "overlaps" by Deborah Tannen (1994). An overlap is not a dominating interruption. Rather it can be a way of establishing connection or support for the speaker. Tannen points out that in order to discern

> whether an overlap is an interruption, you must consider the
> context (for example, cooperative overlapping is more likely
> to occur in casual conversation among friends than in a job
> interview), speakers' habitual styles (overlaps are more likely
> not to be interruptions among those with a style I call "high-
> involvement"), and the interaction of their styles (an interrup-
> tion is more likely to result between speakers whose styles
> differ with regard to pausing and overlap). This is not to say
> that one cannot use interruption to dominate a conversation
> or a person, but only that overlap is not always intended as an
> interruption and an attempt to dominate. (233–234)

The men referred to in the narrative above were interrupting. Interrupting is a form of unnatural silencing.

Other superintendents talked about the discomfort they felt when with groups of men because of the nature of conversations. They reported that the topics of conversations were often not of interest to them or were the occasions for power games. At these times, they chose silence rather than vocal participation. I asked one woman whether she wanted to speak during these conversations. She replied:

A. Oh, heaven's yes.

Q. What do you want to say?

A. If I were to say anything, it would be more kid-centered rather than fiscal-centered.

Q. Men talk more about money?

A. Yes

Q. Anything else?

A. They talk more about politics.

A couple of the superintendents talked about the way their ideas were ignored in meetings with male colleagues. The following is a story about this type of silencing:

> I will have an idea and talk about it. I will say that this is something we need to consider, and no one will say that's a good idea, bad idea, discuss it with me, or dialogue about it. It's sort of like it's just out there. It's on the table. Then they go to the next idea, which they might discuss. So the dialogue about my idea just doesn't happen.

Another type of silencing occurred with some of the superintendents in the study who believed that they had to hide some aspects of expressing themselves. In order to survive, they felt that they needed to hide their emotions. As one articulated:

I tend to hold back emotional kinds of gestures.

Q. Hold them back?

A. Hold them back, yes.

Q. Because?

A. Acceptance. They tend to stop listening to you a whole lot faster if you have some emotionalism in your speech or in the way you express your ideas.

Another superintendent vividly described the need to hide her emotions when she said:

When you swim with the sharks, you can't let them know you are bleeding.

Q. What does that mean?

A. When you are working with a group of people who are out to control or who are into power play, they really like that kind of reflex—one that makes them feel that they are making you bleed. It gives them more power. I think there's a protective element that teaches you learn to control yourself in public. I think if you don't let them know you are hurting, it confuses them. It's kind of like smacking them in the nose you know.

Q. Does that mean that you hide your emotions?

A. Well, I hate to say that, but yes. I don't like having to admit it, either. I don't necessarily think that it is right. I think you should be able—

when you're dealing with people with integrity—you should be able to bleed together, so to speak. But then, it's not a shark versus you. It's not the same kind of water as you're in when you're dealing with sharks.

Clearly, although women superintendents in the study enjoyed the greatest positional power bestowed upon any office in public education, they still experienced overt unnatural silencing. Knowing that this element was a part of their surroundings, that this was the nature of the battleground, was critically important to the women in the study. Their knowledge gave them the opportunity to prepare to handle silencing when it occurred, so they weren't defeated by it. Forewarned was forearmed.

LISTENING AND/OR SILENCE

Although the women in the study admitted that unnatural silencing occurred, they acknowledged that people, in general, usually listen to superintendents. They recognized the privilege of their positions. To make this point, one woman said, "But keep in mind, in a superintendency, you are a voice in your community. So, you are not silenced." Because of their recognition of the power of their positions, they were able to talk about silence with some comfort. Consider how one superintendent talked about her voice:

> I simply say what I think needs to be said and know that my voice will somehow get heard. It may not be heard in the same way another voice might be heard, but it still needs to be heard. And I think that people need other perspectives, and I offer those.

While this superintendent was aware that she might not be heard in the same way as a man, she was confident that somehow because of her position, she would be heard. She was also committed to offering perspectives that were often marginalized. Her mainstream, central professional position as superintendent gave her an opportunity to speak about issues of social justice with the potential of being heard in a way she had never before experienced. She felt good about the responsibility and opportunity to make a difference.

Some of the narrative data centered on the topic of silence were focused on listening—a kind of silence. Women in the study talked about listening as an important part of their communication skills. At times they were perceived as silenced when, in fact, they were listening.

Silence is a requirement for listening. Women are socialized to be listeners, in part, because men and other women, at times, dominate conversations and/or devalue what women have to say. Most of the women in the study used silence (did not talk as much as they would have liked) to be accepted by their male peers, but primarily, they listened—were silent—because they believed it respectful and essential for gaining knowledge. All of the women spoke of the need to listen to people, specifically in order to get input. In triangulation, one participant reflected on this point,

> She looks to the group a lot. Whatever group that may be. If it's a group of teachers, if it's a board subcommittee, if it's administrative cabinet, if it's a parent group, she'll look to the group for ideas, for input.

The ability to listen was, in no small measure, a critical piece of the way the superintendents defined and used power. Collaborative or shared power by definition requires a substantial amount of listening.

One woman stated that others viewed her as someone who was "always ready to listen." She also talked about her natural tendency to be quiet when she said, "I'm a very quiet person. I am someone who really is probably more introverted than extroverted." She elaborated:

> My decisions are usually based on what's best for students and from the perspective of listening to others and gathering as much information about others' standpoints as I possibly can.

Another woman talked about what she had learned by listening to her male colleagues even at times when they were dominating the conversation:

I've learned that by sitting back and listening, I can learn a lot about how male board members function and think. Just by listening to the men superintendents themselves.

Q. What have you learned?

A. Just that there are a whole lot of politics, and they are always very pleasant. And sometimes it's politics for the sake of politics and not politics for the sake of education—one upsmanship—more power control, more power-based, control-based conversation.

One superintendent in the study clearly articulated the benefits of listening from the standpoint of the whole organization:

> I think that the best communication really forces you to listen.
> I think if you build an organization based on good listening . . .
> where cultural communication is no longer an issue. It is no
> longer an issue because you are already listening carefully
> because you care about the person and what they have to say.

In triangulation, I consistently heard that the superintendents in the study were extraordinary listeners. As one person said, "She listens, gets the best out of the people who are available to her."

On one hand, the notion of silence as listening allowed the women in the study to maintain the integrity of their positions and at the same time honor the traditional picture of female as "quiet"—thus, silence as listening was a point of pride for them.

The results of and reasons for listening, on the other hand, go beyond the relatively superficial need for women to feel comfortable as superintendents. Clearly, authentic listening is an important part of superior leadership. The challenge for the superintendents in the study was discerning between the silence required for authentic listening and the silence that resulted from unnatural silencing.

WAYS OF COMMUNICATING TO BE HEARD

Because of the complications around silence and voice, the women superintendents were challenged to come up with ways to be heard because their role required it. Interestingly, most of their strategies had to do with their communication with men—most often male superintendents, board of education members, and members of the business community. Clearly, as superintendents they were thrust into a male culture in the school system and in the community. Consider the comments of one woman:

> I think what I learned was that the rules really change. It gets
> pretty rough and pretty tough, and no one's going to teach
> you the rules. If you're not really fast and really intuitive and
> don't make the first phone call and initiate the idea at the
> beginning—if you're not the first one out of the chute—people
> think you are a loser. And all of my own training and my
> socialization had been to be more respectful, collaborative,
> and collegial. And I think women have to understand that
> men are competitive, to shoot the first ball in the basket,
> throw the first pass, you know steal the first base, whatever it
> is that they do, and women aren't socialized to do that at all.
> And I got it quickly enough. I don't think I got it too quickly,
> but I think I understood quickly enough. I wish I had it more

quickly. I needed to be a lot better prepared in getting out there on issues with men, not with the public, but with the men I had to work with. Specifically, I needed to expect it.

This woman was proud of her ability to "understand quickly enough." Especially since she understood the workings of the world of men—the traditional professional work world of superintendents. She held herself accountable for knowing how the male world worked, going so far as to believe she should have "expected" it even though socialized female. She believed that women should be able to communicate ably when performing as a professional with other male colleagues. She believed that women should be able to meet this challenge.

All of the women in the study had strategies that enabled them to be heard and still be supported by the majority of the people around them. Their narrative data fell into six strategies: 1) Not being direct, 2) Using spokespersons, 3) Careful use of language, 4) Timing, 5) Stepping around egos, and 6) Preparation.

NOT BEING DIRECT

First, the superintendents in the study stated that if they wanted to be heard, they couldn´t be direct in the way they spoke. One woman said, "Women can't be directive or before long they are called bitches." So, in order to be heard, the women superintendents in the study had adopted a "softer style" of communication.

One of the women in the study talked about the dangers for women when they were too "direct" in their speech. Directness in speech was not accepted by men around her. She talked about what she learned in groups made up predominately of men:

You know if you're in an all-male group, perhaps you do not act direct initially. Ordinarily I'm an extremely direct person. But, I will start out initially in a predominantly male-dominated committee or group, not being direct.

Q. And you do that purposely?

A. You know, it's simple because it's a learned characteristic that being direct is not acceptable in that group [all men]. The problem that I have is after I become very involved in what I'm doing, I forget about it. Sometimes I forget the fact that I am being direct.

Q. What are the consequences of that behavior?

A. Oh well, the consequences in a group like that is anywhere from being threatened that you can't get your idea implemented. And sometimes your idea will be redefined out of the mouth of another member of the committee or group and be accepted. But if you are a female, and you are extremely direct, and it becomes threatening to that group, you're not able to get as many ideas implemented as you might if you remembered to play the role that has been given to you [as a woman]. Now that's a nasty thing for a fifty-eight-year-old woman to say.

The evidence that the women in the study were not perceived as having a direct style came during triangulation. One male administrator said, "She is less than direct. It is more of a background substance that she possesses that is not confrontational, not frontal."

USING SPOKESPERSONS

The women superintendents in the study talked about using others (men) as spokespersons in order to have their voices heard. One woman talked about how she used men to speak for her when the mayor wouldn't listen to her because she was a woman:

> The mayor that came in was much more adversarial toward the school district, and the gender issue was difficult. I'm really not sure how comfortable he is working with a woman in authority, so I've tried to utilize the building-and-grounds people (men) to network with him in order to find his comfort level. And there's been much more progressive, positive communication between the two groups lately.

In this particular comment, the woman separated herself from the notion that her voice needed to be used to express her idea. She stated that "the voice was still heard. It wasn't silenced." This separation may have allowed her to discount the fact that someone else's voice expressed her idea and, in the end, may have been credited for the idea. Although I would have categorized the need to have someone else speak for me as "overt silencing," this woman viewed it as a strategy for being heard.

Another woman talked about one of her colleagues who knowingly spoke for her in order that other men in the group would listen to one of her ideas. She told the story:

> I am one of two females in a group of maybe fifty male superintendents. I am also the only female out of ten of us who are the executive committee of the group. In that group

when I have an idea, I will say that this is something we need to consider and no one pays any attention. The group just goes on to the next idea. But there is a superintendent in the group who has noticed this on his own and chuckled about it. So, when he notices it happening, he takes my idea—like one time he actually read it off my paper—and he put it out there. Then it was welcomed and discussed, and that was the direction we went. And later, the two of us sort of looked at each other—and he knew why it had happened.

Another mentioned a similar strategy:

And sometimes the approach is to get other people involved when you know that certain things need to come [from someone else] because that's part of what they want. They become the spokesperson on this issue that we worked on. I get them to be the voice if necessary.

In these comments, the women admitted that the voices of other people needed to be used to express their ideas. For these women superintendents, the most important thing was that their ideas were somehow heard. They were, however, uncomfortable when sharing this information because they knew that superintendents are traditionally allowed and expected to speak for themselves. They understood what Marshall (1985) meant when she stated that "men have been equated with power, while the power women were perceived to have was largely a reflection of the power of the man with or for whom they worked. Women did [do] not have power on their own" (12).

CAREFUL USE OF LANGUAGE

One superintendent in the study reported that she needed to be careful about how she used language. She said that language could have a surprising affect on the all-male administrative team in her district (see Bolinger 1980; Gilligan 1982; Tannen 1986, 1990, 1994, 1995; Wolfe 1994). She emphasized that it was important for her to remember that she was and always would be a female in a male culture (in a sense, a foreigner).

I think that as a woman, I have to be extra-sensitive to what language can mean to other people, other males. In other words, you have to bend over backwards as a female to make sure that you don't confuse men and, thereby, make them uncomfortable. . . . You're not a male. That's never going to happen. You're always going to be a female in that group. It's never *not* [original emphasis] an issue. You're always a female

> in a group of males, and you're never neuter—that just doesn't happen either. So it has to be very, very clear, I think.

This woman believed that if she didn't pay attention to the language she used, men might stop listening, misunderstand, or be distracted.

TIMING

The superintendents in the study knew that the timing of conversations or comments had an impact on whether they would be heard. Consider the timing tactics used by one woman when she was working to be a responsible member of a group:

> When I was first in administration, I found myself mainly in the "quiet persistence" category. All of my colleagues were the "good old boy" type males. That was the way to get an entry—was to attend the meetings. They didn't know how to deal with me. So I found that what was most useful was to sit and listen. Then quietly persist in getting my point across.

This superintendent used the term *quiet* to describe her strategy to be heard. Again, I witnessed the use of a term that alluded to the silencing of women.

Another woman used the same strategy when making the effort to be a responsible member of a group of superintendents. She was talking about the difficulty she had sharing her ideas during discussion. I asked her:

Q. So, what do you do to enable yourself to be heard?

A. Ah, I wait. In a new group, usually I'm not that assertive or aggressive. . . . All the area superintendents are male with the exception of myself and now one other woman. I found what I do is I sit back until I've been with the group for a while rather than try to assert my opinion. I find that I don't speak as often as I would like to when I have opinions.

Q. So how do you decide when to talk?

A. Well, you know I just wait until I've earned the trust of the group. Just a few words here and there. Initially I would choose topics that I was very sure about.

STEPPING AROUND EGOS

This strategy was a difficult one for the women to express. They were embarrassed about the practice and the need for the practice, but admitted that there were times when losing the battle with gender bias meant they could stay around to win the war. One superintendent in the study shared how she had to talk to her board of education so that they would consider what she had to say. She felt it was her responsibility to do so or she wasn't doing her job.

> And I don't know what I can say about how I have to speak differently. I feel that many times I have to sort of "dumb down" what I know, and put it in terms of being able to reach them. That's not true of all boards I've worked with, however. This particular board has a gender issue, and so it's more prevalent.

It wasn't clear to me why "dumbing down" her speech made this woman's board listen to her, perhaps she needed to do this so the men felt superior and, thus, comfortable with male/female interaction. What was clear was that like the other superintendents in the study, she had to figure out strategies and tactics in order to be heard.

PREPARATION

In order to be heard, the superintendents in the study reported that they had to be extremely knowledgeable and prepared at all times, far more so, they felt, than their male counterparts. As one woman said:

> I think that women basically have to talk in the man's world. They have to know it. They have to be almost twice as knowledgeable about any issue because they're challenged more. And their credibility depends on them being able to give answers immediately, whereas, men are not thought of that way. And further, I think in a presentation of my budget, I have to be totally informed and, maybe this is only me, I just feel I have to have it all in my head to put forward and answer immediately. Whereas men don't give half as much in a presentation as a woman does. And they [men superintendents] are believed just as much and maybe more so, because the presentation is made by a man.

Another woman, in a district with a multimillion-dollar budget, had a similar story:

> I don't think they felt I understood what a dollar or a dime meant. . . . I think that women and money are just not conceived of in the same sentences.

Still another superintendent talked about people's surprise when she proved herself knowledgeable. She said:

> You get a lot more questions than men get. But you also get a
> lot of, "Gee, I'm surprised you had so much information."
> You know, it's a shock, but it's common.

Thus, women in the study felt they had to be more knowledgeable of their surroundings than their male colleagues, while, at the same time, some people were shocked when they were.

All of the women in the study were uncomfortable when they revealed they had strategies to counter the silencing they experienced, but they believed that without such strategies, they wouldn't be prepared for the complex difficulties that women face because of gender bias. Some of them even talked about "preparing by practicing" so they could improve their communication skills. One woman reported:

Well, I think women haven't been trained from the time they are young to expect themselves to be the CEO and expect themselves to be demanded from or whatever. I think what is helping women is having small groups of women just sitting and talking.

Q. Do you do that?

A. Yes, I do that. I started that when I first became a superintendent. I am one of four women who get together, and we started meeting like every two weeks, and that was tremendously helpful. We met with a management consultant, that type of thing and as the groups have grown they've been great. And I think you find that a lot of people are doing it now.

Saying that superintendents need to "practice and prepare" in order to be heard may sound unusual, but it demonstrates the determination of the women in the study to move beyond gendered pitfalls.

Some of the women emphasized the responsibility they had for the fact that communication happens in multiple ways. As one superintendent stated:

> I think a real part of leadership is communication in a variety
> of ways. You communicate through behaviors, you communi-
> cate in a variety of ways in order to exchange intangible and
> crucial and fragile information. Do you know what I mean?

Certainly leaders communicate in a variety of ways and awareness of this fact is critical to avoid misunderstandings. And while the women superintendents in the study admitted in discussion that "variety" often meant the ability to be "feminine" *and* "masculine," they were proud that they had developed the skills and strategies necessary to perform their duties as superintendents.

CONCLUSION

Contrary to common sense, the positional power of the superintendency did not eliminate the women's need for gender-related strategies for being heard and communicating effectively. On one hand, it is disturbing to articulate strategies directly related to gender bias because of concerns about reifying that bias. On the other hand, the practices that are being used appear to be a necessary part of the lives of successful women superintendents, and some of these strategies have the potential to transform the superintendency in positive ways.

Further, while I am disturbed that any women have to use strategies of any kind to ward off the effects of bias, I have great respect for the skill, determination, and creativity the women superintendents in the study brought to this onerous task. The women's strategies for communication are evidence that they knew the surroundings when they chose the battlefield of the superintendency.

THE ASSEMBLY

The women of the Assembly reacted first to the word *battle* and what it meant for them in their work as superintendents. One woman began:

> I was hired by a board of education that believed that I had great experience in the battles that they had chosen for me. So, immediately they put three issues on my plate that neither my predecessor nor the board could resolve. While on the surface these issues were closely related to my twenty years of experience, I soon came to understand why they were not resolved. Even my predecessor left because they were not issues to take on. I now advise that you have to do your homework very carefully—understand your surroundings—in order to decide if what is handed you as you enter a district is a battle that should be chosen—especially at first. You can be certain that your first battle will be the one that sets your reputation in the community and makes that very critical first impression. And that first battle needs to be a battle that you know you are going to win.

"I think you are right about the board choosing your battles," agreed another superintendent. "Boards can make it or break it for you if they choose battles that you can't win when you first enter a district."

"I have a strategy for knowing your surroundings as you first go into a district," suggested another superintendent. She went on,

> When I am interviewing, I physically go to the community where I have an interview—prior to the interview. I go to the newspaper office and ask for back issues of the paper. I admit that doing such a thing causes a stir, especially in a small town, when a strange woman comes in and asks for newspapers. But I believe it is important to read the newspaper to see what the battles of a community are and what's going on in the community. Often what you read in the newspaper is a very different picture than what you are given by the headhunter or the board president. You can then see the community from a different perspective. You can also tell what kind of relationship the community has with its newspaper.

"All of that is well and good," countered an administrator,

> but I had an experience that taught me that I could be too prepared. I made the visit to the community and called a lot of people before I went to the interview. The interview was supposed to last two hours, but for me it only took an hour because I had anticipated all of the questions. At the end, a board member asked me a question that obviously wasn't on their sheet of questions. And his comment as he asked it was, "I caught you there, didn't I?" I mean he was shocked that I knew all of the answers. I believe that they thought I was too prepared. That maybe I had gotten a list of the questions or something.

"I've been on the other side of that," admitted a superintendent.

> We were interviewing to fill a principalship. One woman came in very well prepared. And one of the comments from the selection committee was that she seemed too rehearsed, too prepared. We wondered, "How could she know this about us?" So it's really a delicate place to be prepared without seeming that you are right inside the district. People feel like that's invasive or something.

I came to understand that knowing your surroundings and letting others know that you know the surroundings were two different things. Perhaps "knowing your surroundings" also includes knowing that the "surroundings"—the people in a particular culture or community—don't want you to know them too well before they know you, such knowing may feel too intimate for them, like they have been spied upon or something similar. Sensitivity to the surroundings is a piece of "knowing" that cannot be underestimated. And sensitivity suggests that people like their privacy, at least the illusion of privacy. Those hiring a superintendent want to have the upper hand in an interview, so answering interview questions requires more finesse than one might first think. Knowledge of the surroundings helps shapes the responses, but is not necessarily the content for those responses.

"That reminds me of something I have learned," remarked another superintendent,

> And I probably learned it the hard way. I have a tendency to react immediately to things. I had to learn to curb that, because it put me in battles that I had no intention of being in. I gave up my chance to choose my battles carefully when I did that. Especially when people come up to you with ideas or they want a decision from you, you may want to decide because it sounds good or not so good. But you don't know enough to know the surroundings so you can make a good decision. And other people's reactions to the same ideas may be completely different than yours. So, I believe it is wisest to weigh my words and wait before really responding.

"I've had an interesting experience with the waiting thing," responded another superintendent. She continued,

> When someone comes to me, as you were describing, and asks a question out of context, my response is "let me get to know the surrounding first—so to speak—and then I will get back to you." Interestingly, men and women react quite differently to that answer. Men think I have given them an answer, but the women know I want to think about it a while. The men's ideas of my supposed answer, most often, falls into two categories. Some think I said no, and the others think I said yes. So, now I preface my response with the statement, "Now what I am saying does not mean yes or no. Just hold that thought until I get back to you." Using that preface has helped me avoid battles that were not of my choosing.

"I look at this battle thing a little differently," offered another superintendent. She expanded,

> I believe that if you choose to be a superintendent, then the task has been set before you. I see the superintendency as my battleground. Positive battles and even the negative battles that others choose for me are the task. And being a warrior in such a setting involves understanding every little piece of what goes into making a task—all the battles—successful. I approach things from the outside very quietly and then go right to the

heart of it. I stalk the issues. That is why the term "the art of stalking" is an interesting one for me. And it is through my stalking that I come to know my surroundings, know the battlefield.

Clearly, the Assembly's discussion of the First Principle gave fuller meaning to it. Every term grew differently in the mind of the each woman and added richness to the interpretation.

CHAPTER 6

PRINCIPLE TWO

DISCARDING THE UNNECESSARY

To discard everything that is unnecessary is the second principle. . .

—Carlos Castaneda, *The Eagle's Gift*

In order for superintendents to be intensely focused on the best education for all students, they must discard all that is unnecessary so that they are not distracted from the goal. Castaneda, in his book, shared a story that communicated to readers that often when we think something is necessary, we are in some way dependent on it. It is this dependency that makes us weaker. This is not meant to imply that interdependency weakens us, it is just to give the message that warriors must be strong.

When thinking about the meaning of the word *unnecessary* I realized that, for the superintendents in the study, it meant anything that was a barrier to their being superintendents and anything that kept them from reaching the primary goals of their work. And while such a definition is easy to describe, living it was far from easy for the women in the study.

This chapter discusses the things that women had to discard or give up in order to be focused superintendents. Four primary topics, that serve as organizers for the chapter, came through in the narratives: 1) intimate relationships; 2) friendships; 3) privacy; and 4) myths. The first three topics are often mentioned in the literature about the role and lives of superintendents. Because of gender expectations and roles, however, these three areas appear to be even more intense for women. The fourth topic was centered on two gender-specific myths that the women in the study discarded in order to be successful superintendents.

INTIMATE RELATIONSHIPS

The women in the study were aware of the sacrifices they made in order to be superintendents. The most common topic centered on difficulties they faced in intimate relationships.

When I thought through the difficulties that the superintendents faced with intimate relationships, I realized that it was important to note that the women in the study were in their mid-forties to late fifties. Their ages imply that they grew up and were socialized during the 1950s and 1960s. And while I don't believe that the normative values around gender roles have changed substantially, the normative values of the 1950s and 1960s have been fully recorded in the literature on sex roles. This literature is helpful in understanding the values related to intimate relationships that were held by most of the women superintendents in the study. There is information that must be highlighted to help the reader understand the depth of the difficulties the women in the study faced as they lived the second principle.

For example, the phenomenon of the "two-person" career expected the wife to fulfill certain work roles in the home and in public as an adjunct to her husband's work role (Papanek 1973). This phenomenon, which was pointed out in the early fifties, was noted especially among executives' families (Whyte 1956). And, certainly, the superintendent of schools is considered an executive position. In this particular scenario, wives were expected to entertain business associates, keep their husbands healthy and happy so they could do their jobs with few interruptions; and otherwise help their husbands' careers (Blumburg 1985). In the case of a marriage where a woman is a superintendent of schools, most often, complexity is added to the roles of both husbands and wives. To be sure, when a man interviews for the position of superintendent of schools, typically his wife is invited and considered part of the package. When a woman interviews for the position of superintendent of schools, it is expected that her husband has a job and life of his own and that while he may be invited, he will probably not make it to the interview. Certainly, the district doesn't consider him part of the package in the same way.

Further, several of the women told me, with sadness, about their marriages—and in several cases the demise of marriages—and the dilemma facing the men in their lives. Hughes-Chapman (1997, 11) reports that several of the female superintendents participating in her study were living in states or cities distant from their husbands. They had given up the traditional role of wife—wife as living wherever her husband works.

In brief, the women and their male spouses were facing "role conflict" (Gross, Mason, and McEachern 1958; Kahn et al. 1964). The women felt that because of societal expectations, most men had difficulty accepting the fact that their wives were filling the masculinized role of superintendent of schools and often were primary wage earners. They felt that because society expects men to be the major wage earner in marriages, most men had difficulty allowing their wives to fill that role— the "male ego" was a concern. A woman who is a jobholder might not nurture her husband's ego as well as a wife whose only contact with the work world is through her husband. Because of this difficulty and others, for some women, discarding blocks to their success meant letting go of their husbands or partners rather than giving up their careers to save their marriages or intimate relationships.

Many of the women in the study had been through divorces because they had to choose, because of their husbands, between their lifetime desire to have a substantial career and their desire to have a traditional marriage. Many of the women superintendents in my studies, who had faced this difficult decision, let go of their marriages to become superintendents. While I know about a few women who gave up marriages for a career, I will never know how many women let go of their dreams of becoming superintendents to stay in marriages that blocked their career goals.

This topic was an emotional one for the women in the study. They deeply desired close relationships and regretted that our culture has socialized people in a way that makes it difficult for intimate partners (and others) to be supportive of women in powerful positions. This was especially difficult because they not only had a desire for close relationships, but also as women were accustomed to taking the time to nurture intimate relationships. Their jobs as superintendents allowed little time for this seemingly feminine endeavor, and they needed partners who were equally willing to contribute a nurturing element to the relationship. It seemed that they had, in part, given up this piece of socialization. One woman talked about the failure of her first marriage when her husband could not be supportive of her career. At the time of the interview, she was in a second marriage and told the following story:

> I think it is a real key issue whether the man in your life can
> support you in what you are doing. I am in a second marriage,
> and it is an extremely difficult role for a man to follow when

the woman is in the predominately achieving, successful one. When you are sitting in the role of superintendent you have to have a male companion who has a very strong ego and is very comfortable with himself. His (her current husband's) comment was, "I can either sit at home and pout or I can be supportive of you." And he chose to be supportive.

Another woman, also in her second marriage, shared how she "let go" of her first husband so she could live another chapter of her life—a chapter that she would have skipped had she stayed in the relationship. She continued with a story about what she and her second husband had to give up—let go of—in order for her to remain supported in the position of superintendent. She said,

> It's much harder for my husband to sort of change hats than it is for me. I can completely change myself to fit the situation. He is much more into, "I've got to be myself no matter where I am"—which is difficult logic to refute. But by the same token, I try to help him understand that here in this community he can't ever get away from the fact that he is the husband of the superintendent. And so, he cannot express himself in certain ways that he might want to at a certain time. He cannot say things that he would want to. I am sorry. But that's just something we give up.

In this case, role-related expectations of the superintendency had priority over normative ones for being a woman in an intimate relationship. The way the women in the study reconciled role-related and gender-related expectations was to solicit supportive and sometimes altered or culturally unusual behavior from their partners.

FRIENDSHIPS

Other women made statements about discarding notions of what they considered "normal" friendships. One superintendent, for example, talked about the difficulty of maintaining friendships when her professional life was so time consuming. She talked about the patience of friends who continued to call her when she did not have time to reciprocate.

> Although I don't have much time for friends, they are very patient in continuing to include me when it's very difficult for me to make those initiations. They continue to do that.

Another woman stated:

What I think we do is set up our priorities, and if being a superintendent is a priority, we have to do away with other things. And I think we all have preferences when it comes to how we prioritize. I could easily say that I don't keep close friends—having them is something I have given up.

PRIVACY

Certainly, all superintendents give up their privacy when they take the job. Blumberg (1985) discussed this issue in a chapter titled "The Superintendent as Public Property" (171). He states first that "public perception holds that [superintendents are] and ought to be accessible, regardless of time, place or occasion. And second, that somehow, because of both the publicness of [their] position[s] and [their] position[s] as chief among the educators of the community's children, their personal lives should be above reproach" (156). He interviewed only one woman for his book, but found her responses different from all other interviews because "for the first time in our discussion, [the interviewee] seemed to reflect reactions to her job that were based on her being female and unmarried" (157). One of her quotes follows:

> I know I'm a public servant and, therefore, their property. Because of that I have to lead an honorable life, which I think I do anyway. But I can't go out carousing. My social life, I decided, has to be outside of this community. I have to be very careful with whom I'm seen when I'm not at work. I was watched very closely for the first eighteen months I was here. I was even followed by some of the citizens. (157)

Blumberg explains that while the one woman in his sample reacted to being public property in a way that was similar to the men in his study, a very different dynamic was attached to her reaction. He observed two factors: 1) The traditional bias against women causes them to be viewed with "considerable suspicion as they attempt to invade what for most intents and purposes has been a male domain" (158); 2) The woman in his study was unmarried and although it is "all right" in our culture for a man to remain unmarried, many times unmarried women are pitied or viewed with suspicion (159).

As Blumberg noted, the female in his study felt her "public life must be above reproach. And the only way that her social life could be a satisfactory one was to make sure it was removed from her school district. Doubting eyes could not be permitted to see her in other than professional circumstances. It is indeed a fairly heavy burden" (159). Blumberg did not find this different dynamic in the lives of his male superintendent participants.

Interestingly, the married women in my study reported the same "different dynamic" as the unmarried woman in Blumberg's research. Marriage didn't protect the women in my study. Consider the comments of one of the women in my study.

> Anytime that I'm interacting in the community, I am a very public person. There are certain expectations all of the time that you [as superintendent] must reflect the nature of this position and, so, you have to be committed to that in order to just do it. But by the same token, I am very private with my private life and so my husband and I love [the large town close by]. [The large town close by] is a place where you can disappear into the woodwork, and you can, you know, just enjoy those things and be your other private person, too. And we really do that. And you know, thank goodness we can do that.

Other women in the study also talked about the ways that they handled this lack of privacy and possible "doubting eyes." Here is one woman's strategy for addressing this loss:

> I'm probably one of the very few superintendents in this state who don't live in their districts. And it's wonderful because when you go home, nobody gives a rip who you are. You have that privacy that you lose in district. You are able to interact at home in a natural way, to walk your dogs.

While this solution worked well for her, rarely do boards of education give superintendents the choice of living out of the district. It is happening in some locations, however, and may be increasing.

The skeptical reader may believe that men have the same "doubting eyes" evaluating their private lives. I am sure that is true to some extent, but evidently, not to the same degree as do women. For example, Blumberg (1985) quotes one of the men in his study as saying, "Like after a board meeting . . . I may stop with a board member to have a drink" (160). This man made this comment in passing when he was talking about something else. He evidently had no difficulty from the community or anyone else because of this behavior.

Try to imagine a woman superintendent stopping for a drink after a board meeting with a board member. Such an image is difficult to see because women in our culture would be criticized heavily on several counts 1) for drinking, 2) for being out late in a bar, and 3) carousing with a male or female board member. In the Blumberg study, the super-

intendent was probably out with a male board member (for male superintendents, being out with a woman board member would open them to
criticism as well), an act that would definitely be off limits to a woman
superintendent. But, even if she were out with a female board member,
she would be criticized.

When considering the restrictions that women superintendents face
in their public and private lives it is apparent that the women in the
study were devoted to their work as superintendents. Clearly, they faced
losses that all superintendents face, but as Blumberg stated, additional
dynamics for women added weight to these typical losses. Even so, all of
the women were willing and able to remain committed to their professions even under emotionally difficult conditions.

DISCARDING MYTH

There are three prominent myths that the women in the study discarded.
The first is the myth about power and its use—covered in chapter 12.
The second myth is the old idea that any woman in a masculine position
must "act like a man." The third is the myth that a woman's sexuality is
the key to her influence in the male world. Since the first myth is covered
in chapter 12, this section of the chapter focuses on the second and third
myths.

ACTING LIKE A MAN

It is clear that women who have wanted to be managers or administrators have been advised to "never cry" and to dress for success. This
idea is even a part of the literature written for women who are trying to
succeed in a man's world. Consider the following advice:

> To become an executive you must look like what others expect
> a woman executive to look like. Always be understated, never
> flashy. Underplay hips and bosom, don't accentuate curves.
> (Josefovitz 1989 cited in Adler, Laney, and Packer 1993, 11)

Dressing for success according to Jasefovitz meant getting rid of the
female body shape, or in other words, not only act like a man, but also
look like a man. Past research supported the notions that women should
be more like men. Lakoff (1975 cited in Shakeshaft 1989) concluded
that female speech is inferior to male speech, and that women should
develop male language patterns in order to become more effective com-
municators. Shakeshaft added, "Books for women in management told
them that they must communicate like men if they were to become

successful" (184). Without testing this notion, early writers assumed that if it was male, it must be better. McGrew-Joubi wrote that as a result of such information "the first generation of women educational leaders struggled to conform to the male standards" (1993, 45).

The idea of gender-appropriate behavior has over time generated volumes of discussion and research. After all, the separation of people in our society into the categories of female and male is a basic cultural division. Early in life, boys are socialized to "act like boys," and girls are socialized to "act like girls." "This difference in male and female behavior includes a whole set of nonverbal behaviors. Boys and girls learn to sit and stand differently, to gesture in certain ways, to use facial expressions more or less extensively, and to occupy space in different ways. These nonverbal behaviors are strengthened through continuing socialization, so that by the time children have grown into adulthood, they think of these actions as instinctual and natural" (Frieze, Parsons, Johnson, Ruble, and Zellman 1978, 321). Nonverbal behaviors communicate different things because of a shared nonverbal "language" in which certain behaviors acquire specific meanings within a cultural group (Faltico 1969). Part of our socialization is to acquire appropriate nonverbal behaviors and the related interpretive skills. Some behaviors, across cultures, are interpreted as aggressive—the direct stare—and others are seen as friendly—smiling (Ekman 1973; Hall 1959).

Being put in a role that is masculine can be confusing for women. They are faced with the fact that most often they have only seen men "acting" like superintendents. And, the "acting" they do is "acting like a man." The way they stand, sit, gesture, use facial expressions, and occupy space fall in the "male" category of appropriate behavior. So, a woman put in the masculinized position of superintendent might believe that she should also "act like a man." In contrast, the women in the study didn't believe this advice.

For example, they stated that they had to be aware of their style because a "direct" or masculine style was too harsh. One woman in the study said, "If women want to stay in power they have to find a way to circumvent by using a softer style." Another woman talked about the association between "being direct" and being authoritarian, "I'm not seen as being authoritarian or direct. I associate 'direct' with being authoritarian." This reality for women was echoed in the work of Colleen Bell (1995) when she observed that school boards sometimes negatively evaluate women superintendents who are decisive and assertive or "direct."

Interestingly, when describing themselves in a comfortable way, the women referred to themselves as having a "softer style" rather than a "direct style." The word *soft* is a reflection of the speaking style that our culture expects of women.

However, the women in the study acknowledged that their positions as superintendents were most often defined by masculine behavior, and that it was easy to be confused about what type of gendered behavior was expected of them—whether they should behave in a feminine or masculine way. They found a conflict in people's expectations. It was crucial to resolve this dilemma. One woman, for example, referred to her vocabulary and her behavior. At the time, she was talking about being feminine in the role of superintendent. She said:

> You try not to use the language that might classify you other-wise [not a lady] and yet there are situations that all of us are in when our vocabulary is less than we might want it to be. I think a part of being a lady is treating them [men] like gentle-men. The level of expectation for women and men is very clear, that we conduct ourselves as professional men and women in our relationships with others—and it's kind of hard to express—except to say that we're polite. We're [respect-able], by the way we sit, by the way we dress, by the way we conduct our business. We deserve to be respected as men and women of this organization, and we need to model some of those things.

As another woman flatly stated, "Women who act like men: it doesn't work." Once aware of this "truth," the women recognized that they needed to be "comfortable with the fact" that they were women in male roles and continue to "act like women" anyway. Role-related expectations were no more important than gender-related expectations as the strategy for success. As one superintendent put it:

> I believe people who are here [in this position] are comfort-able with the fact that they are women by the time they have reached the position. They have forgone the struggle with believing that they must be thinking like or looking like a man.

Another woman agreed:

> As a woman, I don't want my style to be like a man. I am not a man. I don't think that I would feel comfortable acting like one.

Thus, participants addressed the expectations related to gendered behavior by "acting like a woman" in how they worked and presented themselves to the world. They firmly discarded the myth that women must act like men. They expressed themselves on this topic in a variety of ways.

> I also think that women in leadership roles [her voice gets louder] *must* remember that they are women, and they got where they are because they are women. And we shouldn't act like men.

A second woman shared her reason for believing it important to behave like a "lady."

> And so you know, I think it's also a sensitive thing to the people that you work with that you are simply cognizant of the fact that these are males that have mothers that were fine people. They respect women and they are open to working with, working for women, and you don't alienate that sensitivity by trying to act foreign to that. In other words, behave like a lady [woman].

To be sure, attending to people was an important part of practice for the women in the study. Across my interviews, this behavior was an overt sign to those around them that they knew how to "act like a woman" and meet gender-related expectations. And while one woman stated that all superintendents were expected to pay attention to people, there was general agreement that women were expected to pay attention in a more focused, nurturing way. After listening to all of the women in the study, I came to understand that one reason they succeeded was the fact that they had discarded the myth that a woman in a traditionally masculine role should act like a man.

Interestingly, women in the study believed that "acting like a man" was not appropriate in the public role of the superintendency, but that they "acted like men" in their private lives when they put their careers before the discomfort of their husbands or partners. I came to understand that the public and private lives of the women in the study demanded very different behaviors from them, and it was their understanding of the complexity of these demands that created their success.

SEXUAL INNUENDOES

I learned that one potential barrier for the success of the women superintendents is the idea that women are influential only because of their sexuality. This myth, if not discarded, had the power to damage their dignity, integrity, and credibility. They understood that their presence, because of their gender, in what had been commonly called the "old boy" network created some discomfort for their male colleagues.

Rather than allowing complexity to develop around issues of sexuality, they set ground rules in a simple, straightforward way from the beginning in order to remove any potential threats to their reputations and future success. For example, one soft-spoken woman shared this story:

> If you hold your own dignity and worth, things do change. For example, at the state organization of administrators, another woman and I were the only women—and at the beginning of the conference everyone got up and introduced themselves in a way that made the name of their school as some "dirty" name. At the end of the conference, we talked to the president and said that we didn't want to ruin anyone else's fun, but we thought that as an educational organization, it was inappropriate to use that kind of language. When the next conference opened the president laid the ground rules. . . . Now when you go to those meetings, they are very professional. It was the "good old boy" group—a lot of them were comfortable with it, but they needed someone to stand up and say something.

Another woman recalled a meeting with all men. She said that the president of the group was accustomed to opening the meetings with "dirty" jokes. In fact, the first meeting she attended, the joke was directed at her. She was stunned. Fortunately, two of the men in the group were uncomfortable enough to go to the president afterward and make certain that he didn't continue to tell his jokes. She felt that it was imperative that there be no question afoot about her reputation and communicated that if the men had not stepped forward in her behalf that she would have had to do something herself.

The notion that women are influential only because of their sexuality is dangerous for women superintendents and, indeed, all women. As Cantor and Bernay (1992) remind us, "Ascribing sexual influence to a woman is another way that our society denigrates women's power. Look at all the power Delilah had, yet her power was totally sexual. The story of Delilah is just one example that invites generalizations, such as 'It's really not power, it's just sex,' which put down aggressive women" (80).

The effect of the attitude that women's ability to influence is dependent upon her sexual power has been far reaching. Consider that as late as the 70s, power theorists discussed the influence of women and some men as a category of influence that existed through personal means. Russell (1975) called this type of influence as "power behind the scenes." He concluded that "the qualities required for power behind the scenes are very different from those required for all other kinds, and, as a rule, though not always, they are undesirable qualities" (27).

Certainly, this type of influence has been considered illegitimate and has often been accompanied with remarks such as, "She slept her way to the top." This type of statement or one even close to it, when directed at a woman, completely eradicates a woman's credibility. It is no wonder that the women in the study actively guarded their reputations in extremely stringent ways. They were working to discard, literally wipe out, the myth that women have somehow illegitimately achieved their positions of power. Clearly, this myth stood in the way of their success.

One woman in the study talked about how carefully and consistently she worked to discard this unnecessary and harmful myth from her environment. She focused on how men and women use language differently, and the potential sexual messages that could accidentally be sent if a woman wasn't extremely careful about her use of language. As she put it:

> We use language and yet there's so many different sort of interpretations of both formal and informal meanings of the actual words we use. I think that, my sense is that as a woman, I have to be very extra-sensitive to what those words mean to other people, other males, all the time I'm using them or they're using them because the things that I say, the things that they say, have multiple meanings. And I think you have to not only understand that they could be hearing differently, *you* have to hear them that way and process them that way because that's the way they're processing them. At the same time, you have to work extra hard to make it real clear that there're no mixed messages when you're dealing with really ethical people. In other words, you have to bend over backwards as a female to make sure that you don't confuse men and, thereby, make them uncomfortable and a little less efficient or productive or capable just by putting them in an arena that they aren't quite sure what the words mean and how you're interpreting them. In other words, some of the words that are said, you know, they're hearing them with a double meaning, and it's even okay to acknowledge that, but they have to understand what it does and does not mean to you, as far as the female that they're interacting with. It has to be very, very clear, I think.

Given that the people in her district respected her highly, I concluded that her attention to this myth was time well spent.

The attention to this myth is more evidence that the women in the study understood the complexity they faced when they became superintendents. On one hand, they had to discard the myth of acting like men. They had to remain feminine. Yet, on the other hand, they had to discard the sexual dimension of their femininity in order to discard the myth about feminine sexual influence in professional roles. To say the least, living out these complex nuances required intense attention and focus.

THE ASSEMBLY

The Assembly was thoughtfully quiet after reading the Second Principle. Finally, one superintendent shared an unusual but poignant story. She solemnly confided:

> I have suddenly been given the ability to discard the unnecessary. It is almost like a magic pill I have been given. I was diagnosed with a life-threatening condition, and so now it is very easy to sort out what is necessary. I can say "no" and it doesn't hurt. It's been unbelievable how it frees up all the things that you struggle with that are so unimportant, and you just say "no," and you go in everyday, and you ask yourself, "What is the most important thing today?" You can decide on that very quickly and let the rest of the stuff go. It took some therapy for me to get to that point. It is too bad that we can't get an injection to get to this place, because it really, really has to be part of the job. It helps resolve the stress of the job. I used to be frustrated by all of these choices, but not anymore. For example, today I had the choice of spending some time with some politicians or being here in this meeting. I came here. No contest.

Another women talked about actually discarding her superintendent's hat in order to be a mother to her children. She talked about her strategies:

> I need to make it clear when I have discarded my superintendency role. So, one thing I do is to say the second I walk in the classroom door, "I'm coming here as a mom today." Otherwise they stand and look at me wondering whether I'm there about my kids or that room or whether it has to do with my role as superintendent. So, I am very clear. In fact, I try very hard to dress so it is obvious that when I walk in the door they know whether I am working or not. When I go to parent nights, or parent /teacher conferences, if I can, I'm in

my jeans. That's what this principle means to me. I comes down to what has to be discarded for me to do what is most important to me. It's how you prioritize the bigger things. Not the day to day stuff.

"I think this principle refers to the sacrifices that women make to be superintendents," started one superintendent. She continued,

> I expected to be the perfect mother, the perfect spouse, and the perfect superintendent, and I didn't succeed in two out of those. But I think that we often believe that we have to be perfect in all three of those. And that's where the stress comes from. We have to get a grip on that. The men don't have to be perfect in all three of those areas and we can't resent them for it.

One of the assistant superintendents in the group expanded on the comments:

> When I talk with my superintendent, he never thought about parent/teacher conferences. That was his wife's job. So, it was very clear cut. But, I can't fathom not going. I'm the one who understands what they are learning in the classroom. How could I not be there. Further, if I don't show up, I'm a bad mom or uninterested. But even though I'm the assistant super-intendent and not the superintendent, I still make the teachers nervous. And, I bend over backwards not to. It's just like a no win. Sometimes I think if I took that last step up and became a superintendent it would be even worse. That's hard for me, really a dilemma.

"Yes," another superintendent joined in.

> And if you spend too much energy on the dilemmas that are piling on top of each other you won't survive. It is just so critical to focus and to set those priorities and to conserve energy and let go or discard the dilemmas. Or you won't have enough energy to accomplish the priorities you have estab-lished. You have to make your decisions and move out of the dilemmas.

With this comment, the conversation moved to the area of decisions made. The superintendent who started the shift made an important point:

> We really need to develop the skill of letting go or discarding any anguishing we might do over a decision we have made. Once it is made we have to let go of it. If we continue to process and internalize and anguish over it, that's an expendi-ture of energy that in my opinion we cannot afford. If we

don't learn this Principle, our health, our ability to go on, and our ability to succeed are at risk.

Focus then moved back to difficulties faced in relationships. "I was the first woman to be hired in the region," stated one of the women superintendents,

> and always before when the group had social gatherings all the wives were expected to go off together, and all of the male administrators were expected to go off together. So when I joined the group, I went over and said hello and greeted all of the wives. But, I had some business to take care of with one of the male administrators, so I went to do that. And one of the side comments I heard, as I left the group of women, was, "Oh, I guess she's gonna go join the boys, because that's where she belongs." So, a husband has to learn what to do with all of that, too. Which group should he join? It is a role reversal with which a spouse needs to be comfortable.

This woman had experienced the same difficulties that the women in the study had faced with their spouses. Often there is awkwardness when typical roles are reversed. Partners or spouses have to be very secure people to face the repercussions that result when women become superintendents. Another of the women had similar experiences. She recalled:

> My husband used to go to conferences with me, but he soon found out that there was not a place for him there except to go with the wives. And, he wasn't going to do that. So, he chose to sit in the motel room or he chose to wonder around the hotel. Eventually, he said he wasn't going with me because there was nothing for him to do. So, it was something I had to give up—my wanting him to be with me so I could be part of a couple at dinner in the evening like everyone else was. It was a desire I had to discard. Giving up having him with me goes hand in hand with being a female superintendent. For whatever the reasons, there are sacrifices in every nook and corner.

"Well, that stuff about giving up friendships is certainly true," added another administrator. She said,

> So, I have made a decision that I will continue to bowl with my women friends on Wednesday night. I don't give it up unless absolutely necessary. I protect that night. I do the same for my husband and stepchildren. I schedule in a night. Because I am very concerned that I'll look back in ten years and ask, "Where did it all go?" So, I guess it would sound strange to say, but bowling is my life, and it has to be.

The statement "bowling is my life" is symbolic for this woman. She found a way to view her friends and family as necessary to her success so they didn't have to "discard" them—although she admitted that her time with them was limited by her work. The notion that to discard anything that is unnecessary may, in the minds of some, assume that work is the most important priority. While listening to the Assembly, I came to understand that priorities needed to be established within the scope of whole lives, not just work lives. And yes, there were sacrifices on all fronts, things had to be discarded on all fronts, and one of the fronts was at work. Some of the things at work had to be let go of or discarded.

The conversation later turned to the myth about "acting like a man." One superintendent shared a personal story about consequences she faced when she crossed the line. She recalled:

> Early in my career when I was going through an interview for a superintendency, I was being shown around the district and I opened a door for a male board member. As soon as I did it, I knew I was finished. I could see it in his eyes. It was all over for me as far as my candidacy. The same board member had a fishing and hunting conversation with my husband. I knew enough by that time not to enter that conversation, but it was too late. I learned from that situation that I couldn't act like a man.

There was agreement around the room that "acting like a man" just didn't work.

CHAPTER 7

PRINCIPLE THREE

CHOOSING BATTLES

Aim at being simple. Apply all the concentration you have to decide whether or not to enter into battle, for any battle is a battle for one's life. . . . A warrior must be willing and ready to make his [her] last stand here and now. But not in a helter-skelter way.

—Carlos Castaneda, *The Eagle's Gift*

Through his story about Don Juan, Castaneda (1981) conveys to readers that complications many times draw us off our central purpose and leave us confused. Don Juan advises warriors to "aim at being simple." Women in the superintendency talked about keeping things simple by choosing their battles carefully, even when securing a position. One woman talked about her attitude toward seeking jobs and staying in them once hired:

When I go for something, I go for it wholeheartedly. I've never applied for a job and not gotten it. I don't want that to happen. Pick the battles you can win. Then when you win, the first thing you need to do as a new superintendent is pick a tough issue that you know you can win, and win it—so people see you as a winner. But you need to study and decide which things you can win!

The women in the study stated that they kept their agendas very simple, saving the clout they had for the battles that really mattered to them. Especially in the beginning stages of administration, they were more silent than most superintendents because they found that women were initially given less credibility than men. They saved energy for what they referred to as the "important issues." Take, for example, the way one woman made sure that her male colleagues listened to her.

> For example, I would say, "We talked about doing so and so, and if we should do such and such." And I would repeat what I wanted to say—persistently pursue—what I thought was important. It is a case of choosing your wars carefully.

One of the women took the idea of choosing battles carefully even further when she drew attention to battles that can't be won during one's professional lifetime. She talked about these battles:

> Some of us have to choose the battles that we know we won't win during our tenure as superintendents. And I hope that after me there is somebody with the heart, skill, and intelligence who will take that battle on, because I'm not going to be able to do everything that needs to be done in this battle in my time as superintendent. I'm going to make some headway. But I chose this battle knowing that the battle is bigger than I am. Somebody's got to step up and take the tough ones. And if we don't get started on the tough ones, it's not going to be good in the end for any of us. This type of battle is one that we're going to be in the whole time we're in the job. We may be doing some other battles that we are winning, but that core battle for children is being waged from the moment we take the position, and it's not over when we leave the position.

While the application of the Third Principle varied, one theme dominated the narratives. In culling through the interview data, I learned that the twelve women participants repeatedly emphasized how they had simplified their work by focusing on their primary purpose for being in the position. that primary purpose was children. One woman discussed how she simplified the demands of the job in order to minimize other superficial or trivial tasks so she could address the needs of children.

> I have found that my world has become reduced to very few intersections in a very narrow channel in a very limited world view as superintendent. All of the intersections have different names—the groups, the committees, the problems, the task, the whatever. They're all different issues superficially, but at a deeper level, they are all the same.

This woman could focus on her primary concern—children—because she organized the bulk of her administrative work under that category. This simplified her agenda and kept her purpose uncontested.

All of the women in the study gave intense energy and attention to the lives of children literally "in their care" in their districts. Their natural caring was focused most intensely on the well-being, both academically and generally, of the children. One superintendent discussed the main focus of the district as related to children:

> When you talk about [our] school district, you can say it is a school district that really believes in the individual human potential of every child preserved. And you hear that reflected in the way people talk, but you also see it in what they do. There is a congruency there. What they talk about and what they live. . . . The values that we have are those that the community has for its children.

For the women in the study, the focus on children was a prominent and essential requirement for success in their roles as superintendents. Battles done for children were directly tied to their success. For example, one woman, when asked about success, spoke initially in terms of improving the lives of children. Many of the women noted that they believed they focused on children and curriculum/instruction issues much more than any men they knew or had worked for in the past. They recalled that the conversations among men at national meetings most often centered on finance and facilities. To be sure, research has revealed a severe lack of attention to curriculum and instruction issues by superintendents (the vast percentage of whom are men) (Bredeson and Faber 1994).

In contrast, I came to understand that the women in this study believed themselves and other women to be much more involved with curriculum and instruction because of its direct relationship to the lives of children. Many stated that their own success in their position was closely related to the outcomes for children. When discussing success, one woman did not refer to herself; rather, she defined her success as something contingent on the educational success of the children in her care.

> I measure success by the fact that 73 percent of the kids in our city graduated from high school the year I came, 81 percent graduate today. I measure success by the fact that we have many alternative schools where kids are getting degrees now instead of being out on the streets or in the jails. I don't feel successful because too many youngsters who have not been successful in academic areas are minority youngsters. I am still having real difficulty in getting our people in our elementary schools to believe that poor youngsters can learn. . . . I worry . . . about the children—somebody's got to be responsible.

This particular aspect of caring was highlighted by Gloria Ladson-Billings (1995), who argued that "Collins's (1991) use of caring refers not merely to affective connections between and among people but to the articulation of a greater sense of commitment to what scholarship . . . can mean in the lives of people" (474). The women in the study were intensely focused on the academic achievement and the general well-being of the children in their districts. This caring attitude was expected of them, in some part, because they were women.

A CARING SUPERINTENDENCY

Caring as a simple focus is not easily accepted. It is a carefully chosen battle. In fact, a caring attitude as required for educational administration is currently receiving attention in some of the literature (Beck 1994; Purpel 1989; Sergiovanni 1994). And while this literature advances what I believe is a worthy message, there are bureaucratic barriers to caring in schools. The bureaucratic barriers come in the forms of hierarchy in power relationships, standardization, and uniformity (Darling-Hammond 1984, 1988; Ferguson 1984; Helsel and Krchniak 1972; McCall 1995). These barriers seem to discourage caring practices in teaching and administration. A system that puts the thoughts and values of administrators above those of the teachers and the children is not a caring system.

McCall (1995) points out that although teachers often are overtly caring toward students in their classrooms, the administrators do not act in caring ways toward the teachers. She concludes that when administrators act in oppressive, authoritarian ways, they are modelling behavior that is not caring. For teachers to teach children to be caring and for them to be caring toward children, they need to be treated with care as well. Thus, for administrators to be caring toward children, they must be caring in all their relationships because equal treatment of all is a piece of caring behavior.

The twelve women superintendents in the study valued relationships of all types. They cared about the people in their districts and in their communities. This comprehensive view of caring was also directed at the children in their districts. And as is evident in this chapter, their caring for kids was their first priority. Further, their first priority was consistent with their behavior towards adults. They were working in ways that removed some of the bureaucratic barriers to caring. With a caring superintendent, it is possible for the system to change for the better (Brunner 1998). It is appropriate in such a system to treat others—administrators, teachers, parents, community members, students—with respect and care.

The women in the study had concentrated intensely and chosen their worthy goal, their worthy battle. They were willing to take their last stand over issues related to children. Thus, they choose an ethic of caring for their professional interactions at all levels because they understood that such an ethic is not defined as something to be bestowed on one group. Only if they cared for everyone could they care for children. And as one women said, "Kids are the last stand." The superintendents were not "helter skelter" when they made this decision. In a profound sense it made their work "simple," but certainly not easy.

THE ASSEMBLY

"I think the process of getting 'into simple' is very, very complex," warned one of the superintendents. "Each decision that I make is a battle for my professional life, whether it is a small decision or a large decision. And, I think it is more so for me because I am female, and because I am black. I try to come from what I believe is my primary purpose and the reason I do my work. . . . And I understand very clearly that it could be my last stand."

"I hear that!" erupted a principal. She continued with the following story:

> Last night I had a conversation that when it ended the other person threatened, "You won this one but you won't next time!" I was shocked. That part of the principle that says "not in a helter-skelter way"—well, it certainly was that. I mean, I didn't think the situation was a battle when, in fact, it was. And it was definitely helter skelter. And I think it upset me so much because I didn't think of it that way at all. I will be aware from now on and be more careful.

"I agree that it is an incredibly complex task to keep simple the role of the superintendency and the choosing of battles," added another superintendent. She continued,

> I think that it is incredibly complicated, and to do it I pull from all of the experiences I have had in life personally and professionally. It is my experience that helps me anticipate the eventual result. Further, I think that the ability to take a stand and come out of it with a positive result is directly related to

the skill of choosing which battles to enter and keeping them as simple as possible. Now that's complicated!

Another woman joined the fray, "As a superintendent I use the rule 'Keep It Simple.'"

She added,

> Every time I knew I was about to get into a big fight over something, I'd say to myself, "Okay, just stand back and keep your eye on the ball." And, the ball is the kids, and whether they're going to learn something from this. Whether this will benefit their learning. That's the ball. And then if somebody is arguing with me over whether or not soccer from the community can play on the football field, it wasn't a big issue. But if the issue is going to impact the kids and their learning, then it becomes a battle. And yes, even a battle to the death. You know, a warrior must be willing to take that last stand, because it's that critical.

There were nods of agreement around the room. Then one superintendent was openly puzzled about the deeper meaning of the principle when she said:

> I am having trouble with the coherence of sentences that make up the principle. I am comfortable with the idea of keeping things simple. And I can be comfortable with the second part with it saying that you have to "decide your battles," because we can't make everything a battle, you can't have everything be an issue. And the part about a warrior must be willing and ready to make her last stand. Yes, we need to do that, but that's part of choosing the battle. So, I guess that sentences two and three seem to go together. But the idea of helter skelter throws me. The helter skelter thing comes at you from the strangest places because an issue for one person may not be one for another, and that causes confusion. You just are thrown into battle sometimes.

"I agree with you that sometimes we are just thrown into things," asserted another superintendent,

> but, in my opinion, going to battle isn't even a decision. It's a mission. It's that mission that we all have been talking about— educating kids and making sure that they become our next generation of leaders. I think the helter skelter thing occurs because people don't have the same mission. Our mission as superintendents is our passion for kids. If we lose that passion, we lose focus. And if we lose focus, the decision-making process becomes helter skelter and the battle is lost.

Another superintendent had additional thoughts:

> I see that helter skelter thing as a reminder of the preplanning that is necessary. And, of course, you can't anticipate everything. But to think through what could possibly happen in the process is important and to anticipate whose issues may come forward as you're approaching something, I think is important. And to have a way to address the issues for the time being is important even though the details of the issues may not be crystal clear. It seems that if the helter skelter component becomes a part of the works, then the whole purpose of the group is derailed.

"Yes, in fact, I have found that helter skelter can be a strategy for those who have a different agenda," offered yet another savvy superintendent. "At times, when I have been working on social justice issues, working for the disempowered or the abused or the assaulted, whoever has the power advantage is ready to make it a battle. What seems simple to me in terms of its importance becomes "fighting words" to those with a different agenda. And then those with a different agenda use helter skelter as a strategy to derail whatever work is being done."

I found this piece of narrative particularly insightful. The idea that the introduction of helter skelter energy could be used as a strategy to stop projects or other important work was helpful to the women as they thought through various ongoing battles in their districts. Certainly the interweaving of simplicity, taking a stand—particularly one focused on children—and avoiding doing these things in a helter-skelter way were vividly familiar to the women of the Assembly.

CHAPTER 8

PRINCIPLE FOUR

TAKING RISKS

Relax, abandon yourself, fear nothing.

—Carlos Castaneda, *The Eagle's Gift*

Castaneda, when talking about the Fourth Principle, recalls a moment when, because of difficult conditions, he could not organize his thoughts. His midsection was in knots, so he took deep breaths in order to relax. At that point, his teacher praised him and reminded him of the Fourth Principle. Castaneda came to understand that unless he could move to a state of relaxation where he feared nothing, he would not be able to move in the direction of the unknown (280). He would not be able to take such a risk.

In fact, according to Cantor and Bernay (1992), "Risk taking is a critical factor of successful leadership" (158). Warren Bennis (1989) agrees. In his list of characteristics of future leaders the reader finds, among other things: "Willing to take risks" (41). Most management and leadership books acknowledge the necessity of risk taking as an attribute of leadership.

What about the literature on educational leadership? To be sure, there are some researchers, such as Short and Greer (1997), who write about how important it is for administrators to support innovation and risk taking. They do not, however, report that administrators themselves are risk takers. In fact, other literature reports just the opposite. School administrators have never been portrayed as risk takers (Konnert and Gardner 1987).

Superintendents, too, as a part of the larger group of educational administrators, are not reported to be risk takers. In addition, research shows that superintendents, in general, "regard themselves as 'hands on' mangers more than visionary executives constantly seeking for alternative ways in which to make their school organizations more effective. The ingrained adage 'let's not reinvent the wheel' often appears to create a climate militating against creativity and risk taking" (Carter, Glass, and Hord 1993, 25)

When reviewing the literature on superintendents, I found very few references to risk taking. More specifically, there were no references to risk taking either on lists of superintendent competencies or on lists of desired personal attributes. Consider a study by Haugland (1987) that identified the professional competencies and skills required of superintendents. The study established one list of competencies perceived as important by school board members and another list perceived as important by superintendents. The lists were ranked in order from the most important to the least important competency (41).

School Board Members' List	*Superintendents' List*
personnel management	superintendent/board relations
school finance	personnel management
curriculum development	public relations
accomplishing board's goals	school finance
superintendent/board relations	accomplishing board's goals
public relations	curriculum development
policy formulation	policy formulation
school construction	school construction
collective negotiations	collective negotiations

Risk taking is not on either list nor is it among other researchers' selection criteria for superintendents. Miklos (1988) lists the following personal attributes as important in the selection of a superintendent: judgment, personality, character, open mindedness, physical and mental health, poise, intelligence, sense of humor, voice, and cultural background (54). Powell (1984) and Robertson (1984) list other criteria as necessary for superintendents: understanding how the school board operates, and how the board and superintendent relate; management of the budget and financial resources; and developing relationships with parent and community groups.

One final example of the type of attributes desired and perceived to be important comes from a study done by Sclanfani (1987) of 1,800 superintendents. Eight performance areas containing fifty-two skills emerged from the data. The eight performance areas were: climate; district finances; development of an effective curriculum; creation of programs of continuous improvement; management of district operations, delivery of an effective means of instruction; building strong local, state, and national support for education; conducting and utilizing research in problem solving and program planning. Risk taking was not among the fifty-two skills identified under the eight performance areas.

Other literature on the superintendency rarely mentions risk taking. One section that discusses "collaborative risk taking" can be found, however, in Susan Moore Johnson's (1996) book about superintendents. Yet she does not refer to superintendents as risk takers; rather, she suggests that superintendents enable collaborative risk taking in others in order that innovation take place in classrooms (146–148).

Further, Konnert and Augenstein (1990) have a chapter titled "The Superintendent as Assessor and Alterer of Risk-Taking Propensity," in their book, *The Superintendency in the Nineties: What Superintendents and Board Members Need to Know*. In that chapter, Konnert and Augenstein observe that "the outcomes of decisions are never entirely predictable. The element of risk is always present in varying degrees. . . . It is obvious that decision makers vary in their propensity to engage in risk-taking behavior" (95). The intent of their book chapter is to help superintendents decide whether they and others around them are risk takers. In addition, they discuss how to change risk-taking behavior. They note that a study by Brown (1970) found that business administrators are more willing to take risks regardless of age, experience, or the size of the organization than are superintendents (Konnert and Augenstein 1990, 97). They conclude with the following caution: "It is important that the element of risk not become the overriding factor in educational decision making" (99). And while I believe it is important to note that risk taking just for the sake of risk taking could quickly lead to disaster and serve no positive end, the importance of the ability to take risks seems to be overshadowed by Konnert and Augenstein's messages of caution.

A further discouragement for superintendents is the fact that the context of the position does not often support risk taking—one thing implied by Konnert and Augenstein's cuation (and indeed supported in the literature: see Blumberg 1985; Cuban 1976; Carter and Cunningham 1997; Johnson 1996; Tyack and Hansot 1990).

Why, then, a chapter about "risk" as a part of successful practice for superintendents? Simply, because I found the theme in the narratives of the women in the study. The comments made by the twelve women superintendents on the risks faced and taken, revealed that risk taking was a large part of their professional practice. Further, I learned during triangulation interviews that people who observed the superintendents' professional work considered them risk takers. In fact, many people believed that to be in the superintendency in the first place is a significant personal risk for women—that they have no choice but to be risk takers.

RISK AND FEAR

Why is risk taking an important part of leadership? Warren Bennis (1989) and others point to the fact that without an ability to take risks, creativity and innovation disappear. And certainly, creativity and innovation are critical for problem solving, change efforts, and developing strategies for improvement. Paula Short and John Greer (1997) agree. In their review of the literature on teacher risk taking and innovation, they cite many studies (see Amabile, 1983; Berman and McLauglin, 1977; Getzels and Csikszentmihalyi, 1976; Hall and Griffin, 1982; Hennecke, 1991; House, 1977; Leithwood and Montgomery, 1982; Lightfoot, 1986; Little, 1982; cited in Short and Greer, 1997) that reveal and advance a variation on the theme "that a climate of experimentation and risk taking has a positive impact on school staff trying out new practices" (72). They end their review with the definitive statement, "Risk taking is critical if new ideas are to emerge in schools" (73).

Certainly, any change is in itself a risk. And, as Susan Moore Johnson (1996) writes, "[l]eadership is about change" (146). Thus, for change or reform to occur, leaders of any reform must be risk takers.

What, then, is risk? "The word risk comes form the Greek 'to sail around a cliff,' which implies that we don't know what's around the bend" (Cantor and Benay 1992, 165). What would it take for us to sail around a cliff when we didn't know what was there—to move into the unknown? Because most people fear the unknown, it goes without saying that moving into the unknown takes a type of fearlessness. Not the fearlessness that comes from recklessness or foolishness, but the fearlessness that comes with self-control. Without this type of fearlessness, a person would never "sail around a cliff." She would live in fear.

Fear, in the view of some, is a sickness that blocks the healing necessary for us to be whole beings. And as with all sicknesses, fear seems to be involuntary; something beyond our control. But for many different reasons, the women in the study had a type of fearlessness. That did not mean they had no fears. Rather, they seemed to understand that they were responsible for their own fears. In fact, they made it clear that being responsible for their own fears involved a change of mind before behavior could be different, and they were willing to change their minds. For example, a mind centered solely on job security could disallow them the ability to take risks, and most of the superintendency literature focuses on job security. The superintendents in the study had changed their minds about the need to primarily focus on job security and focused instead on the lives and academic achievement of children. They gave up their fears around job security when attending to issues related to children.

One of the ways they changed in their minds to become more fearless came from their ability to achieve the first two parts of Principle Four, "Relax, abandon yourself. . . ." They had life circumstances and personal characteristics that helped them to relax and forget themselves. The most important of those circumstances were: 1) community, and 2) challenge. The most important of those personal characteristics were: 1) courage, and 2) curiosity. The combination and interaction of all four helped them relax, forget themselves and gain a type of fearlessness. And it was their fearlessness that gave them the freedom to take risks, to be creative in their work. Certainly, creativity is a necessity for women superintendents. Their very survival in the position depends on it. And creativity is thwarted without risk taking.

To be sure, as with other things in their lives, they were curious about their own risk-taking tendencies. One woman talked about her thoughts:

> Women who are superintendents have to be by their very nature a little bit more risk takers than the general population of women. . . . Their risk taking tendency wouldn't let them avoid things because I'm [they're] always out there. I'd say, ya, let me try that! My husband and I were just talking about this, and I asked him, "Do you think I'm a . . . risk taker. What am I in all of that?" He said, "Well, I definitely think you are a risk taker or you wouldn't be doing what you are doing."

Indeed, as noted by this superintendent's husband, all superintendents take a risk when they take the job. But for women the risk is even greater.

The remainder of this chapter is organized in the following way. To begin, in four short sections I share narrative that reveals the two life circumstances and two personal characteristics that helped the women in the study to relax and abandon themselves. Next, I briefly discuss the results of the women having these two circumstances and two characteristics in their lives. The chapter ends as the others do, with the voices of the Assembly.

TWO CIRCUMSTANCES AND TWO CHARACTERISTICS OF FEARLESSNESS

THE LIFE CIRCUMSTANCE OF COMMUNITY

The term *community* as used in this section is defined as any type of supportive environment. The women superintendents in the study were aware that they received help, in myriad supportive environments, to develop their willingness to confront fear and change their minds. For many of them, the support that nurtured their ability to control their own fears came from prominent people—fathers, mothers, grandfathers, bosses, and mentors. One woman reflected on the source of her attitude:

> It comes back to whether you are willing to risk anything. . . .
> My father used to say, "Why not?" We'd say, "Could we do
> something?" And he'd say, "Let's give it a try."

In fact, their fearlessness about moving into a position that is most often viewed as "off limits" to women was inspired by people in their lives who told them they could do anything. Being female was not presented to them as being a problem. As one woman said, "I never thought about gender as a reason I could or couldn't do something."

Some of the women in the study were in families in which all of the children were girls. It appeared that fathers, in these cases, in the absence of a male child, treated their female children—especially the oldest girl— the way they might treat a boy. There is no way to know whether the same fathers would have treated them differently if there were male children, but it was clear when talking to these women superintendents that their fathers treated them in ways that expanded rather than limited the women's views of what they could do in life. And this treatment helped create their belief that they could become superintendents regardless of their gender. As one woman said:

> I am the oldest of four children, and I always have believed in
> the impact of the father/daughter relationship. My father said
> you can do or be anything you want, and I mean I set my goals!

In *Women in Power*, Cantor and Bernay (1992) have a chapter titled "Empowering Messages to Give Your Daughters." They begin by stating that one of the most important contributions of their research was the "identification and analysis of the . . . enabling messages" that women in power received as children. They hoped that these messages would be used by readers to empower their own daughters.

Cantor and Bernay identified that girls have two parallel "Dream Tracks." Those tracks are the traditional bride/mother track and the ambition/career track. Each of these tracks is built by the thousands of messages that flow back and forth between parent and child during the growing years. The daughter takes these messages into herself and organizes her personality accordingly (228).

The depth to which girls take these internal messages becomes even clearer when considering the research of Carol Gilligan (1982). Her research illustrated that girls define themselves through relationships and connections, thus making the things they learn in relationships, with parents or important others, profound in determining the course of their lives. The traditional track of bride/ mother comes solidly through to girl children.

However, the career track is not inherent in traditional mothering or fathering. Research has shown that when given an equal opportunity to watch both men and women, girls tend to watch women more often and boys tend to watch men more often (Maccoby and Wilson 1957). This research suggests that behavior learned through observation is divided along gender lines, making the traditional bride/mother track strongly predominant in young girls. This is not to say that the traditional track is bad, rather that without some overt experience with the career track, the women in the study might not have become superintendents.

Without a doubt, more women are working than were working in 1957 when Maccoby and Wilson did their research, so it could be asserted that girls growing up today are watching mothers who also work or have careers. But, the women in the study, who were raised in the 50s and 60s during the time of Maccoby and Wilson's research, in the main, watched mothers who did not work outside the home.

Further, as is evidenced by the narratives of the women in the study, women are still doing the majority of the traditional work that is done at home. So girls still get the message that housework is women's work. They may get messages about careers more often, but they continue to get the message that women do housework rather than men.

Without a doubt, career track messages need to be deliberately conveyed to girls (Cantor and Bernay 1992). The women superintendents in the study had received the messages of the career track, and most times they received them through relationships in family or other intimate community. Cantor and Bernay list five messages to empower girls. They are:

1. You are loved and special.
2. You can do anything you want.
3. You can take risks.
4. You can use and enjoy your Creative Aggression.
5. You are entitled to dream of greatness. (230)

Most of the women in the study had received some form of these messages from prominent people in their lives. Only one of the twelve women didn't grow up in an environment that contained these messages. Her story was quite the opposite. She grew up with adversity, and her success came because she chose to succeed in spite of her background. She refused to fail. And when people in her life told her she could *not* do something, she did it anyway. As she put it:

> I still don't like being told that I can't do something. I want to prove to people that I can do anything that someone says I can't.

Further, the same woman had a daughter, and she understood the need for different types of messages for her daughter than the ones she received. As she said:

> With my own daughter, I am trying not to raise her the way I was raised. I try to instill that she can have a career.

In some cases, belief in God and being part of the community of believers helped the women in the study let go of their fears. Their beliefs helped them abandon themselves while they put their trust and lives into the hands of a being they believed much larger than themselves.

THE LIFE CIRCUMSTANCE OF CHALLENGE

One of the messages that the women superintendents in the study communicated to me was that they sought challenges. It was as if they needed to test their own mettle in difficult situations. And, certainly, being female in the role of superintendent was a challenge. But these women wanted even more challenges once in the position. Perhaps once a challenge was met, a new challenge was desired. And without a doubt, the role of superintendent of schools offers many challenges. One woman said,

> I like the fun of solving really intractable problems with very difficult people. There's a part of me that finds that very appealing. It's really a challenge, and it's really important when making a big organization work. You must be able to work with difficult people and complex problems. I like that. I like the responsibility actually. It feels good.

Another woman told me how she had really enjoyed being superintendent in a large district of 60,000 students and was there for some time. But when an opportunity arose for her to take a position in a very difficult district that was more than twice the size, her desire for a challenge won her over, and she took the job. As she said, "I just really wanted to see if I could do it."

There was talk from the women about other types of challenges the superintendency afforded them. Interestingly, the idea of failure as a positive challenge came up at times. If a woman avoids experiences because she is afraid of failure, she gives up many opportunities to test her own knowledge. Gelb (1998, 87) asks the question: What would you do differently if you had no fear of making mistakes? What would you learn? As one woman put it:

> Failures are just a matter of time and circumstances when you are a superintendent. Boards change and issues change. The situation is always fragile. There is no way to be assured of success all of the time. Failure is just a part of the picture. So, you have to understand that you grow from failure just as much as you do from success. And that's the challenge, to keep that in mind.

Another woman compared herself to what she called a "maintenance superintendent." She was referring to the traditional superintendent profiled earlier in this chapter. She revealed her comfort with challenges when she said:

> Most superintendents, I think, don't want to rock the boat, ever. They want to be in a long-term position, so they never make any changes. They may put out a fire here and a fire there, helping situations in ways that keep them in power and in their jobs. They want to be safe. They keep the boat [the district] afloat. But the ship may never go anywhere, it just drifts. To make changes, you end up in a rocking boat. And that's where I live—in a rocking boat.

This woman was comfortable with challenges. She and the other women in the study expected challenges and would be bored without them. As Don Juan said, in Castaneda's (1967) book *Journey to Ixtlan: The Teachings of Don Juan*, "The basic difference between an ordinary [woman] and a warrior is that a warrior takes everything as a challenge while an ordinary [woman] takes everything as either a blessing or a curse" (Fields 1994, 3).

THE PERSONAL CHARACTERISTIC OF COURAGE

The women in the study had the courage to step into an unknown masculine space, and that is not a small thing. But even more interesting is that fact that once in the position, they continued to take courageous stands on issues that typically are very risky for superintendents. Courage was a characteristic of all of the women in the study, and it seemed to be connected to their ability to abandon themselves. For example, listen to one woman's story,

> Dad came home one day with a new tractor, and we all went out to see the new tractor. While we were out there, we turned around, and the house was on fire. My mother ran back to the house. In the house was my sister who was just a baby. Mother was burned severely getting my sister out of the house and was in the hospital for over three months. And when she came out of the hospital, I remember them saying that she would never play the piano and things like that again—but she did you know. And there wasn't anything she couldn't do. If you look with courage and say here's the difficulty—I always said that if you were a one-legged man, you could hop, you know. Courage is to know that few things in life are fatal.

Another woman expressed her idea of courage in a similar manner:

> I just ask myself, "What's the worst thing that could happen." And then, I move on.

The women in the study understood that courage is not evident unless difficulty or adversity is present as well. One time when the women in the study had to be courageous was when they faced the common obstacles that women face when seeking jobs as superintendents. The literature points to various obstacles for women seeking educational administration positions such as lack of support from networks/mentors, the absence of role models, attitudes toward power and leadership, and family demands (Brunner 1995; Edson 1988; Grogan 1996; Hill and Ragland 1995; Marshall 1989; Regan and Brooks 1995; Schmuck 1975, 1982; Shakeshaft 1989; Tyack and Hansot 1990). All of the women in the study, as is revealed in other chapters, courageously faced all or some of these common obstacles as they moved into administrative ranks. They worked through and went beyond them.

Another area where the women in the study had the courage to take difficult stands was around issues of social justice. As issues related to gender, race, class, disability, and sexuality come to the table in school districts, superintendents who take firm stands are often faced with dismissal or serious losses in terms of support. These issues are not an overt part of the superintendency literature. Most times, they are relegated to the arena of "what's legal." Questions such as "How do you make certain that the district is in compliance with state and national mandates?" drive the discussion rather than any serious effort to change attitudes about bias. Such compliance issues generally show up in personnel or special education literature rather than in the educational leadership literature.

For the women in the study, however, these issues were more personal. Certainly, the fact that they faced gender bias as they negotiated their way into the superintendency gave them experiences that shaped their attitudes toward equity. Moving outside social norms is perhaps the quickest way to understand that bias exists.

In contrast, I have seen accounts where women in positions of power publicly state that they have not faced gender bias. After talking with a couple of these women, I have come to understand the depth of danger women face when they admit experiences of gender bias. The women in my study, however, as with the women in other studies (see Astin and Leland 1991, Chase 1995, Grogan 1996), perhaps because of the safety of anonymity, told many stories of their experiences of gender bias. And as I point out in one article (Brunner 1998), "[i]t is important that people understand that gender bias does not disappear when women are in positions of power" (179).

Thus, the personal experiences the women had with bias created their need to put issues of social justice on their agendas. For example, one woman talked of two or three instances where she was prepared to risk losing substantial support for the sake of hearing all voices and honoring equity. One issue in the community concerning diversity actually pitted her against the majority of her board. She argued:

> I really saw it as not letting a minority of people who have
> this elitist attitude make a decision for this community. . . . So
> I now have five members on the board who are not happy
> with the fact that I opened it up.

What drove her in this case was her belief that the students benefited from the inclusion of all perspectives. An example she provided was "developing programs and doing work with the inner city." Despite the lack of encouragement from a major sector of the community she moved ahead with the plan. As she said:

> I am going ahead with it because, truthfully, students of this community really do need to have other insights and other views, learn to live with others and understand differences. So we're moving ahead with that.

She admitted that "those are the kind of decisions that limit the tenure of a superintendent in a particular district." Even faced with a limited tenure, she had the courage to take a difficult stand on an issue of social justice.

Finally, the women in the study had the courage to be self-reflective. For example, all of the women were excited by my research project, first and foremost, because they believed that they could learn something about themselves. They had the courage to see my view of them as I interpreted their narratives. They had the courage to face themselves.

How does a person face the mirror of self-reflection? Gareth Morgan, in his book *Imaginization: The art of creative management* (1993), has a chapter titled "Looking in the Mirror." In the chapter, he discusses exercises that help people see themselves both through their own eyes and through the eyes of others (26). He suggests that "all of us operate out of some kind of image of who and what we are. All of us project images, most of which have both negative and positive consequences. If we can come to understand these images, and how they coincide and collide, we have an enormous resource for improving the impact of what we do" (26).

As I understand it, the women superintendents in the study learned more about themselves because of the project. Indeed, because I interview people as a part of my work, I have come to understand that many superintendents are not interested in having an outsider ask employees what they think about the superintendent. And this is not true just for superintendents. I believe that most people have discomfort about such questioning. Some, as I have experienced, even put a stop to it.

The women superintendents in the study had the courage to face themselves, to face their fears, to take difficult stands on issues of social justice, and to face and overcome the obstacles to becoming superintendents in the first place.

The Personal Characteristic of Curiosity

Curiosity is built on the natural desire to learn more. Kenneth Clark (1993 cited in Gelb 1998) describes Leonardo da Vinci as "undoubtedly the most curious man who ever lived," and as someone who, "wouldn't take Yes for an answer" (50). Da Vinci's curiosity insisted that he study everything from multitudes of perspectives, for it was through multiple perspectives that he gained a deeper understanding of whatever he was studying (53).

The connection between curiosity's desire to understand and the need for multiple perspectives to create that understanding is the hallmark of a lifelong learner with an open mind. Further, the need for multiple perspectives when seeking understanding opens the seeker to diversity and difference in a genuine, authentic way.

Such was the curiosity of the women in the study. While it would be easy to say that their attention to social justice issues was strictly related to their own experiences of gender bias and to the fact that they were noble people who wanted to do the right thing, these statements would not catch the complexity of their involvement. In part, they listened to multiple perspectives because they wanted to understand them. They were curious. They wanted to know whether the thinking they did was different or like that of others, and they wanted to understand how and why.

Curiosity about experiences also propelled the women superintendents into the unknown masculine world of the superintendency. They wanted to walk in the shoes that didn't necessarily fit their gender. And that walk around the corner into the unknown is a more mysterious one for women than it is for men who move into their first superintendency. For men, just seeing other men do it makes it a more knowable and imaginable trip. Women do it in the dark with their hands tied while wearing shoes that don't fit. Without strong curiosity, I doubt that women would take that trip. When one woman in the study told me that she just wanted to see if she could do a particularly difficult superintendency, I came to understand that her curiosity about her own ability to function within a particular experience, along with her love of challenges left her with no choice. She had to take the position—a position that most would not even think about taking.

Finally, and perhaps most important, the curiosity of the women superintendents in the study, which made them life-long learners, also made them the best of models for education and learning.

THE ASSEMBLY

The women of the Assembly began their discussion focused on the first word of the Principle—"Relax." One of the superintendents started:

> I find that when I have what I think are the biggest problems, if I relax, sit back, and ask myself, "What if. . . . " then I begin to realize that those problems are not problems, but rather they are just situations. That is when I am at my most creative. And things begin to occur to me that never would have previously. . . . Knee jerk reactions just aren't as good. So, the relax and abandon yourself, to me means to mentally abandon yourself so that you can face the situation in a positive way.

Another superintendent saw something else in the principle:

> I like this one because for me it is an invitation. It's saying, "Hey, do it! Go for it! Don't worry about it. You think it's right? Do it!" It's an invitation to take that risk. I look at it, and I go, "Yeah! I would follow that principle."

One of the superintendents was reminded of some research she had read. She added:

> When I read Principle Four, it reminds me of some of the things we've learned in brain research about the "flight or fight" instincts—those are the primal instincts that we have when we're engaged in battle. When we are using those primal instincts, we are at our least rational. We are less able to reason. But when you relax, you move your thinking functions to the frontal lobes—the portion where we reason and reflect. That is when we are able to be creative in problem solving. So, the advice is good for kids on the playgrounds as well as people sitting in the superintendent's chair.

Another superintendent added further wisdom to the conversation:

> I agree that if you can relax and abandon yourself, and if you feel that you're doing the right thing, go for it. But, I think there's more to this principle. That is, if you can also, when working with other people, get them to feel relaxed with you, the creativity that comes out of the whole process is even greater than when it just involves one person following the principle.
>
> I have found that in working with people, if I am relaxed and others are relaxed, the results we get are much better than if I'm the only one that's relaxed. If we can somehow convey to others to let their hair down, that they're able to assume the role of risk takers, and that they know that you're not

writing everything down, but it's just a good easy conversation where all the ideas flow. This type of conversation leads to good consensual decisions many times.

One of the women administrators brought up the topic of culture and how it affects a person's ability to relax. She said:

I think that culture has a lot to do with whether you are able to follow this principle or not. For example, I think when you are new to a culture, you are much more tentative. After you are more established, a level of trust begins to develop that will allow you to make mistakes, so you can take risks. That is when I am more likely to take risks and allow those around me to take risks. Currently, I am very lucky. I have a board who will verbalize when they're happy with something I have done. Their positive statements give me room to make mistakes and not feel as if they're are judging me on that one action. I know that they have approved of or appreciated other things I have done. I have an overall record of doing things that they are happy about. That makes taking a risk okay because I have a cushion to fall back on.

And as far as helping others be relaxed, that also takes time. The people have to know that I won't judge them negatively if they make mistakes

Clearly, this woman understood that becoming a part of a culture takes time. She was also aware of how much we depend on our connections with the people around us when we are wanting to be our natural relaxed selves. And while she made an excellent point, it reminded me of the "chicken and the egg" dilemma. Just who starts this atmosphere of risk taking?

In this case, the woman was not a superintendent, she was a central office administrator. So she had more hierarchical bosses than do superintendents. Her comments were a heavy reminder to all of us just how difficult it is to suspend hierarchical or positional power. This seems to put the weight of modelling risk taking on the shoulders of those at the top. But then, where is the top really? Superintendents answer to the board, and boards answer to the voters, and some voters have more power than others outside of the voting booth. This particular line of thinking brings me back to the realization that there is no real place to begin such an attitude except with myself. And that seemed to be the attitude of the women superintendents in the study. They were risk takers from childhood because of the four circumstances and characteristics in their lives and within themselves.

The discussion of Principle Four finally came to rest with the idea that perhaps one aspect of relaxing, abandoning self, and fearing nothing could be around making the decision to leave a position or even the career of superintendent of schools. One woman, who was not a superintendent, listened rather than talked during the session. She finally spoke up:

> I have been thinking about all this talk about fear and risk taking, and for me—as someone who might want to be a superintendent someday—it is pretty scary to hear this stuff. My first reaction is to go home and start over and try something new. But maybe my attitude ought to be just the opposite. Maybe you've got to relax, and just let it be, because you never know what you're going to face. I guess the message for me is that I have to just sit back, take it all in, and finally decide whether the life of a superintendent is what I want after all. And if I don't want it, then I need to leave my current job and do something else. I certainly don't want to be afraid of all of those people. And I don't want fear to get in the way of my own personal life, and I certainly don't want to be afraid every day as I go to work. So, if I can't let go of fear, I guess I can't do this job.

A superintendent added:

> What you say is also true once you are a superintendent. If you are in a situation where you can't relax and let go of fear, then you probably need to move on. Sometimes it's a matter of fit in that particular district. Sometimes, it might be the superintendency in general. Maybe the role is not for you.

To be sure, evidence of marginalization and isolation, overt and covert forms of gender discrimination, and diminished personal quality of life for women superintendents in a male-dominated role has been found in several research studies. Further, gender politics exacerbate the challenges of an already complex and difficult leadership role. These experiences influenced some women occupants to leave the position (see Beekley 1996, Tallerico et al. 1993, 1996).

"Tallerico and Burstyn (1996) argue that such unpromising contexts contribute to the premature exit of qualified women superintendents, reflect an ingrained system of gender stratification, and reinforce the continued disproportionate formal power of men in the superintendency" (Tallerico 1999, 38). Their research echoes Marshall's (1985, 150; cited in Tallerico 1999, in press) conclusions about women in male sex-typed careers in general: some women may be "rejecting a patriarchal, political, manipulative model of school leadership . . . seeing [such models] as disconnected to the core technology of schooling."

Principle Four seemed to cover a multitude of situations, from hiring to exiting, for women in the superintendency. The women of the Assembly found its message a meaningful and profound one.

CHAPTER 9

PRINCIPLE FIVE

SEEKING RETREAT

When faced with odds that cannot be dealt with, warriors retreat
for a moment. They let their minds meander. They occupy their
time with something else. Anything would do.

—Carlos Castaneda, *The Eagle's Gift*

Castaneda wrote that at one point in his warrior training he could not
focus on a particular topic so he got up and began to look around. He
began examining the furniture in the room and even the buff-colored
tiles that made up the floor. One of his trainers praised him for retreating
for a moment by letting his mind meander. Castaneda was practicing the
Fifth Principle. He was faced with odds that he could not deal with, so
he retreated.

To say that anyone in the superintendency is faced daily with difficult odds is almost an understatement and well confirmed in the literature (Blumburg 1985; Kowalski 1995; Moore Johnson 1996). To find a
way and place to retreat, then, is critical for anyone in the position.
Retreat as a part of the practice of the women in the study was pursued
in at least three ways: 1) as a way to relieve stress and remain physically
healthy; 2) as a strategy to be prepared for situations of all types; and 3)
as a way to take a rest from the gender-specific difficulties that do not
exist for men. Retreat in these three cases is not even vaguely related to
defeat. Instead, such retreat is fiercely attached to remaining in the fray,
in the position, with renewed strength. The first two can be found in the

literature on the superintendency (Carter and Cunningham 1997). The third is specific to women.

The necessity of retreat for superintendents came home to me when I asked what one superintendent's secretary would do for the superintendent if she could. Her heartfelt answer gave me pause. Practically in tears, she replied that she would give her five minutes alone in her office. She said that five minutes was far more than the woman ever had to herself. Clearly, retreat time is not easy to find.

When telling about this part of their practice, the women appeared to be slightly uncomfortable. It seemed that this aspect of their lives was almost too private to reveal. They were so accustomed to measuring their worth by their "on-task" behavior that they seemed hesitant to admit that life held more than focused work. When they began sharing the information, however, it was clear that they considered retreat space vital to their well-being, and, for continuing to excel in their positions. One woman revealed the following:

> I need time for myself in order to think and to heal, and I call it being out in nature and just enjoying the trees and the bees and whatever else . . . I think that that's very important and it's a way of renewal. And retreat in the sense of only rebuilding strength and courage and for clearing out your mind.

Retreat for the purpose of regaining strength was a necessity for all the women in the study. Similarly, Hill and Ragland's (1995) research on women in educational leadership positions concluded that the women took time for stress-relieving activities. The women superintendents in this study found ways to retreat in the midst of their busy lives. Some of the women talked about how different they were when they were retreating from the work world. One woman expressed it this way:

> [T]he private self is a totally different self. I mean you get a little schizophrenic. . . . I am very private with my private life, and so my husband and I love to go to a place where you can disappear into the woodwork, and you can, you know, just enjoy all of the things it has to offer. You know, enjoy those things and be your other private person, too.

Another said:

> You have to be a chameleon sometimes. It has nothing to do with being two-faced to people. It has to do with the private self, and what you're willing to expose of your true feelings, and risk the vulnerability of that kind of self-disclosure. And I won't. I'm very guarded about myself, as a person.

The strategy of preserving the inner self from absorption into the professional role can be found in the accounts of lives of women in other professions. Consider, for example, what academic Linda Winfield (1997) wrote:

> I would often (at least in my own head) make a conscious and deliberate distinction between my profession (or what I do) and who I really am. This allowed me to have some semblance of a "self" that operated independently of my profession. . . . This distinction . . . allowed me to exist in a reality larger than academia and thus avoid acquiescence to mainstream academic values or to alienation. Whenever I encountered disappointments, rejection, marginalization in academic pursuits—and it occasionally happened—I was not totally devastated, because my sense of who I was was not entirely dependent upon being accepted and rewarded by my peers and colleagues in academia. Conversely, when chaos and confusion occurred in my personal life, I shifted to the professional realities of my existence, and to my spirituality. (195–196)

The retreats or breaks from the mainstream of professional life provided space for the women in the study to get back to themselves, to remember who they really were. Castaneda (1981) relates that warriors, at times, are confronted with so much new or confusing information that retreat is critical. In times of retreat, warriors do anything that takes their minds away from the confusion of the moment. After taking the respite, warriors are ready to move quickly with sureness—they have regained their sense of purpose and self.

For some, like Winfield, belief in God provided solace and a touchstone for remembering what is most important in life. Their beliefs helped them relax or retreat to a deep inner level—a type of relaxation that is often overlooked in our culture—and be themselves. They could be who they really were because they put their trust and lives into the hands of a being they believed much larger than themselves. It appeared that, from at least one woman's perspective, even her placement in the superintendency position was a part of a larger deity's plan for her life. As she shared:

> I believe that I need to do the very best I can do right where I am, and the good Lord will let me know if I'm supposed to be somewhere else.

It was clear that many of the women had given careful thought to the "type" of retreat time they needed. One superintendent talked about several different types. First she talked about private time with her family.

> There's the time for getting away with your family. . . . Part of that kind of time is to make sure everybody is away from things they normally do so that we really have some time together.

Next, she talked about the type of private time she needed to "come back stronger" on the job.

> The district just sent me to Harvard for two weeks, and that was really time to reflect and think. There's a need for finding time to really think about what we do and reflect about it, write about it [undirected, on your own time]. There's a need to spend time reading what's current, thinking about what's current and almost getting my whole belief system and value system sort of regenerated. And, yes, that time is definitely harder to find than vacation time with the family or time with the family.

Finally, she talked about the type of "retreat time" she needed to stay physically, emotionally, and spiritually healthy.

> I need some down time. And I run for that. Before I became a superintendent, I ran ten miles every day. And then with that first superintendency it had to stop. And one of the things I've learned from stopping is that there definitely needs to be time spent for me on my own. I think it's truly just knowing that we come back stronger. We think clearer when we take care of our bodies as well as our minds. And for me it has to be a solo activity for it to work.

This woman was very aware of the types of retreats she needed to remain healthy in her job as superintendent. Her health was an instrumental part of her ability to face the "impossible" situations in her work world. Further, as can be inferred from Castaneda's book, retreat is a part of the warrior's training. As a Principle of Power, it is as important as any of the other six principles. It must be practiced along with the other principles or the warrior never reaches a state of impeccabilty nor experiences the three results of impeccable practice—which is how warriors solve the riddle of the heart.

Actually, a warrior would welcome opportunities that create the need to practice the seven principles. Certainly, being a woman in the position of superintendent creates plenty of situations in which to practice the seven principles. In fact, just being female is an experience that most superintendents (at least 90 percent are men) haven't had. For example, I have come to understand that one experience that women have that is unlike their male counterparts is the biological fact of menstruation and menopause.

What does menstruation and menopause have to do with the Fifth Principle? I realize that this may be a stretch for the reader, but what I have learned from the women superintendents is that the experiences of menstruation and more specifically menopause taught them lessons that prepared them for living the Fifth Principle. Any woman understands the retreat that she enters into when she is menstruating. It is a time of withdrawal into herself that is accompanied with an increased sensitivity to the relationship she has with the world.

The lessons of menopause are similar. Lynn Andrews (1993) talks about these lessons—lessons that are taught to female shaman or as Castaneda calls them, warriors. She states that the first lesson of menopause is that we are alone—this is one state of retreat. Menopausal women understand the innate feelings of isolation and separation because the menopause passage is one they experience alone. Changes in their responsibilities around their children—when they have had them—also create feelings of aloneness. Retreat is a space of aloneness, a space where isolation and separation become a positive experience.

The last lesson of menopause, according to Andrews, is that we are truly all one. This is the lesson that is learned after living through the retreat process. After time away, the warrior comes forward ready to connect with the world in a stronger, more sensitive, and more aware state.

Why is menopause, in particular, a part of this chapter? In large part, as well as menopause's connection to the Fifth Principle, the answer is related to the age of the women when they enter the superintendency. Research done on the career paths of women in education (Ortiz 1982) reveals that most enter administration positions later than do men. Accounts of women in the superintendency report they rarely enter the position before their middle to late forties, and many enter during their early to mid-fifties (Gupton 1998). Career paths which have often accommodated the raising of children may be an important factor determining when women become superintendents, but other issues may play as important a part. Carolyn Heilbrun (1988) points to other possible reasons that women may wait to become superintendents:

> [S]he has become braver as she has aged, less interested in the opinions of those she does not cherish, and has come to realize that she has little to lose, little any longer to risk, that

age above all, both for those with children and those without them, is the time when there is very little "they" can do for you, very little reason to fear, or hide, or not attempt brave and important things. (260)

This is not to say that all women superintendents have already raised children, but certainly a majority of those in this study had. Further, all of the women were at least in their mid-forties. Most were in their fifties, a time of life when women face the biology of menopause.

The absence of discussions about menopause both in the literature and by the women in the study is not surprising. First, the role of superintendent of schools has been perceived as a male role, making moot any point about menopause. Second, most often the attitude toward menopause is negative. Our culture tends to treat it as a disability or even a disease, something to be diminished with medication. Thus, women avoid discussing it, especially in professional arenas.

No one wants to be seen as less able in a position, and women, who are already working against odds, do not need another reason to be deemed less capable. Few have escaped the story that the reason a woman cannot be President of the United States is because she might suffer either premenstrual syndrome or "hot flashes"—both of which would render her incapable of rational decision making. In fact, "in the early 1970s a controversy arose when a physician on the Democratic Party's National Priorities Committee publicly asserted that women were unfit for high-level executive jobs and government offices because of their physiology, particularly the menstral cycle and menopause" (Frieze, Parsons, Johnson, P. B., Ruble, and Zellman 1978, 191). Clearly, women have reason to avoid talking about menopause, and this avoidance is in itself a gender-specific "impossible odd" facing women superintendents that men in the role do not face.

Because this book is grounded in the wisdom of another culture, it is appropriate to look at menopause from a different perspective. Women in all positions should be able to discuss all issues of physical well-being—especially issues that are common to all women.

The women in the study were not unusual. They did not readily or openly talk about "feminine health" issues. On occasion in private, I heard a comment, generally accompanied by light laughter, related to menopause. For example, one woman stated, "We don't call them 'hot flashes,' we call them 'power surges.'" This statement, in various forms and in various settings, was repeated to me several times and is evidence that the women superintendents were looking for a different way of thinking about and talking about menopause.

Lynne Andrews, in her book *Woman at the Edge of Two Worlds* (1993), offers a perspective on menopause that I believe is useful, and it recognizes a type of retreat/sacred space for women. Andrews relates her experiences under the guidance of her two Native American elder teachers, Agnes Whistling Elk and Ruby Plenty Chiefs. Her teachers taught that

> menopause is the gateway into the most sacred time of a woman's existence on earth, a time when she can at last discover the deeper meanings she has sought. And yet, this rite of passage is usually silent, an unspoken of and mysterious journey. We joke about our hot flashes in an attempt to make them less frightening. We have no idea that these symptoms of shifting hormones are also the kindling of a fire within that prepares a woman for an incredibly powerful time of life. . . . The change of life is a time of release when a woman begins to reap the benefits of all that she has learned and done . . . a process of rebirth from which a woman emerges with new responsibilities, new mirrors, and new power. (2)

Andrews asserts that power is gained from the retreat provided by menopause and, yet, realistically, she also acknowledges that although women in today's world are more frequently gaining positions of importance, the negative connotations of "women as aging" continues to create a feeling of loss, particularly in regards to looks. And it is our looks, we have been taught, that give women power. Ancient cultures used to value the wise old sorceress. Today such a woman is thought to be just an ugly old witch. Sadly, the wisdom and other attributes of older women are lost in our culture.

In contrast to our cultural norms, Gloria Steinem (1994) writes about the many attributes of older women. She suggests that women have the strong potential to become more radical as they age because of the loss they feel. They may think and do things they never could when they were younger (261). She recognizes the newfound time and freedom that older women gain as they lose their youth.

In the same vein, menopause can be viewed as providing newfound time for retreat and freedom. In fact, it is a type of retreat in and of itself because it signals that child bearing and most often child rearing is over. Certainly, the fear of unwanted pregnancy—which while it has lessened because of birth control methods, still remains a factor—is over. And while the passage of child-centered years is bittersweet, more women than not react positively to what has been referred to as the "empty nest."

Women whose children have left are more satisfied, less self-pitying, and less easily hurt than women whose children are still at home (Lowenthal et al. 1975). In fact, they generally show fewer depressive symptoms when their children are independent of them (Radloff 1975). Beyond these positive changes, the "empty nest" suddenly releases a great deal of time to women. Since women still do most of the childcare in our culture, when that is done, they have newfound time on their hands. And for the professional career woman, such as those in this study, this newfound time gives more space and flexibility to their extremely tight schedules— a "real" space for retreat.

It appears that the experiences of the Fifth Principle are inherent in the experience of menopause—a parallel phenomenon that creates a surprisingly natural training ground for women wishing to be warriors. Significantly, the women in the study gave me the impression that they used all of their experiences—including menopause—in order to do their work as superintendents. And by including in this book an open discussion of one of the many biological attributes of women—menopause—I hope that it can be recognized as retreat space and be acknowledged for the strength and rebirth it provides.

THE ASSEMBLY

"This guy, Castaneda, is a brain!" exclaimed one superintendent. "All of this parallels exactly what we're learning about how the brain functions best. It functions best in a relaxed state where there isn't stress that causes it to shift down to the brain stem thinking—which are the primal instincts. And in that frontal lobe, in that cerebral area, is where we're the most creative, the most dynamic, the most flexible, where all of the parts of the brain are interacting with each other!" In brief, she indicated that stress was something that needed to be minimized for optimum brain function— certainly something important for any superintendent. And if retreat was a source of stress reduction, then it was a necessary and essential part of the job.

Thus began the Assembly's discussion of Principle Five. It continued with comments and questions about the private and public self. One administrator asked:

> Do others of you feel that there is a piece of women superintendents that never comes out, that nobody ever sees except

in private? And is that necessary? And is it different if you are
new to an area or if you grew up in an area?

"I'll answer that," offered another superintendent,

> I think that it is absolutely true. I can't say that the people in
> the community that I am in right now see the whole picture,
> see all sides of me simply because it is me. The raucous side of
> me probably is the most inappropriate for a superintendent to
> exhibit. But, I have a mean sense of humor, and it is just not
> acceptable conduct. And, I do, I have a terribly mean sense of
> humor. But it's not something that I would let many people
> see because it's not an expectation of the position.
>
> On the other hand, we can let our hair down with our
> families. But again, something like flippancy, some of the
> retorts that you'd love to give, you just don't because it's not
> acceptable behavior. . . . Do we ever get past that? Maybe if
> we spend a long time in a district. It's about trust and com-
> fort. But even if you grew up there, and you have a little more
> history, I still think there's always a piece that we hold back.

Another of the superintendents joined in:

> I think all of us have to have a public persona. After all, we
> represent the school district to the wider public. So there's
> some responsibility that goes with that. Yet, any of us would
> be happiest if that public persona was an integrated and
> congruent part of our private selves. Otherwise you have a
> schizophrenic kind of life—one is the public side and then
> after eleven o'clock at night you step out of that and put on
> your pajamas and then you have the private life. And that's
> hardly a way to live.
>
> So, your public life has to be congruent enough with your
> private life that you feel connected and whole in both. And I
> don't know how gender related that is—the dichotomy. I
> would imagine that it crosses all kinds of lines: racial, gender,
> and everywhere people feel the need to develop a public
> persona.

"Maybe," suggested one of the administrators,

> length of time in the position helps one become comfortable
> with the role. This talk about being alone sounds so much like
> when I started out as a principal seventeen years ago. I felt I
> could not be friends with the staff that I helped supervise. I
> wasn't able to be myself. But now I have grown so much into
> the role that I am very different as a principal. Now I feel I
> can be myself with a staff and am comfortable with it. But I

remember distinctly saying to myself, "Don't be friends with
people with whom you work."

At that point, I asked her if she was still in the same school district. She
answered:

> No. This is my third district, fourth school. I certainly have let
> a lot more of those boundaries go. Maybe I'm not as good a
> principal as I was in the beginning. But I had tons of fears. I'd
> like to hear from people who have been superintendents long
> enough and are probably more comfortable in the role.

One of the superintendents spoke up:

> I've been a superintendent for ten years in three different
> districts, and I feel comfortable in the role. Yet I haven't been
> able to let my hair down in any of those settings because of
> the expectations of the role—not because I just didn't want to
> let it down. I felt restricted by how a superintendent is sup-
> posed to be. And the expectations of what a superintendent is
> supposed to be was different in each of the three districts.

As the discussion continued, it became clear that the women believed
that retreat was a real part of their jobs. They turned the focus on different ways they "retreated." One superintendent shared:

> I may retreat in a different way than others because in the
> small district I am in, I am the superintendent, the principal,
> the business manager, the transportation director. You name
> it, I do it! I didn't realize until now what I have done.
>
> When I moved to the district, I changed the office around
> so that a screen sits diagonally between me and my office
> door. My office door is always open so people can walk in.
> But, the screen gives me a moment before they can get to me. I
> can collect my thoughts, can realize who's there. I have given
> myself a way to retreat. Some people find it very disconcerting
> because they can't see exactly what I'm up to! But I do retreat.
> And I retreat behind my actual screen. And it gives me those
> few seconds that I need.

"I think I've learned to do an 'on the move' retreat," started another
superintendent,

> and I think I tend to do it by pulling out of the conversation.
> I'm a very loquacious individual by nature, too much so
> sometimes, even for my own comfort level. I mean I used to
> feel as though I had to respond—you know what I mean—so
> that there was never a dead spot in a conversation. I was one

of those compulsives about filling that dead spot. And I've gotten to the point now, where, especially in a group of people, by pulling out of the conversation that I have moments of retreat. I don't feel a compulsion to react to everything. I just let the talk go on around me and it just gives me a time to pull back a little.

Not that I don't hear what's going on. I'm there, and I'm tuned into it, but I'm tuned into it from a different level. I'm not tuned in as needing to respond right then. I'm almost so to speak in another room with my mind so that it relaxes my head, I guess. I almost have to do it deliberately sometimes, especially if it's a confrontational situation, the intensity of it builds and I don't want to react in a way that is not characteristic of me. So I need time to regroup. I don't want to speak off the top of my head. I want to speak from a position of thought—it isn't always possible. So I do this kind of retreating from within the context of conversations or circumstances that are going on.

"I do much the same thing, I guess, by frequently saying that I need time to think about this or that," added another superintendent. She continued,

And my staff knows it. They know that when they spring stuff on me they can't expect an immediate answer. I say, I need time to think about this, I'll get back to you, or come back to me. And during the first year it was hard for them, but they've gotten used to it now.

An administrator confessed:

I actually count. I know it's dumb, but I got it from sitting in a dentist's chair. I put my mind on hold and just start counting. And when I'm really frustrated, I joke with people and say that if I'm counting to a million, there really is a problem here. It really calms me down. Maybe it's like counting sheep!

Clearly, the women of the Assembly understood the need for retreats of all types—"anything would do." The conversation brought to the table a part of their practice that was rarely articulated, much less discussed.

CHAPTER 10

PRINCIPLE SIX

COMPRESSING TIME

Warriors compress time; even an instant counts. In a battle for
your life, a second is an eternity; an eternity that may decide the
outcome. Warriors aim at succeeding, therefore, they compress
time. Warriors don't waste an instant.

—Carlos Castaneda, *The Eagle's Gift*

When I first read Principle Six, I immediately thought about tasks needing
to be finished in a shorter amount of time than is ordinarily needed for
the same task. I thought in terms of compressing tasks. But since the
most important tasks in the superintendents' work lives could not be compressed, they had to figure out ways to truly compress time as Castaneda
suggests.

The American Heritage Dictionary of the English Language (1981)
defines "compress" as: "To press together or force into smaller space;
condense, compact" (274). Under the words "compressed air" is the following definition: "Air under greater than atmospheric pressure, especially
when used to power a mechanical device or provide a portable supply of
oxygen" (274).

When I looked at the definition of "compressed air," I began to
think about compressed time in a new way. If compressed air is "air
under greater atmospheric pressure," then perhaps compressed time is
time under greater than usual environmental pressure. That works. Time
for superintendents is under greater than usual pressure. Further, if

compressed air can be used as power to make things happen, perhaps compressed time can be used in the same way.

To be sure, the women superintendents in the study were cognizant of the dilemmas they faced when they had to decide how they would spend their time—with whom they would take the time to talk and listen. One woman in a large district shared her frustration:

> I've found [the problem of time] to be a major problem in the size district [large urban] that I have. When you're talking about [so many] kids and [so many] employees, and the demands that are made on your time by the social groups within the district, the business groups, the community groups—whether it's about integration, the union, overcrowded schools, lack of financing, old schools. . . . You must decide as superintendent who will get most of your time. If you're politically savvy, you'll give it to the top businessman . . . [or] to the school board . . . because they hold your job in their hands. But if you spend your time where you want to, working with small groups of principals, meeting with teachers after school, then it leaves less time for the others. So, it becomes a real battle.

Every instant counted in this woman's life. Further, she and the other women in the study understood that they were in a battle that affected many lives—decisions made about where and how much time they spent with particular people or on certain issues were ones that determined the outcome of their own lives and the lives of others in their districts. Most important, the way they spent their time made a difference for children in one way or another. This critical battle determined that the women in the study learned to practice Principle Six. They learned through life experiences to compress time.

COMPRESSING TIME AS A PART OF PRACTICE

Compressing time became a necessity for all of the superintendents in the study, first, because of the nature of the position, and second, because of the additional components of their lives and professional practices that are unique for women. One superintendent talked about the extreme and constant need to compress time—about the fact that she didn't have a moment to waste when she said, "I work fifteen hour days constantly. I have no life other than work. None." This particular statement could be viewed as a complaint, but it was preceded by her statement that she "just loved" her work.

What does it mean to have no other life than work? Castaneda (1981) talks about the warrior as one who applies the seven basic principles of the Riddle of the Heart to "whatever they do, from the most trivial acts to life and death situations" (291). Within his description is the basic understanding that for a warrior, "the work" is constant from the most trivial acts to life and death situations. Such a statement could be made about spiritual work, in general, and the work of the warrior is just that—heart work, spiritual work. Thus, a statement such as "I have no other life than work" could just as easily be stated as "I have no other work than life." The latter statement, in my view, is how the women in the study viewed work—it was life.

But such abstract solutions are easily suggested. Pressing questions remain. How did the women approach life/work in the practical sense? How did they compress time in order to succeed? The rest of this section describes three primary ways that the women superintendents in the study compressed time: 1) Doing more than one thing at a time; 2) Thinking about more than one thing at a time; 3) Viewing the role as one relational thing to do; 4) Understanding the patterns of uncertainty and ambiguity.

DOING MORE THAN ONE THING AT A TIME

One way that the women in the study compressed time was to do a lot of things at the same time—or more accurately during the same time frame: talk on the telephone, make notes on a memo, and file things. This particular practice is reported in other literature on women administrators. It is something that the women in the study had done all of their lives. They reported that they had always been extremely busy and had ceaselessly accomplished far more than anyone else they knew. One woman gave an example from her past:

> During my senior year, I was the person who got the awards for participation in more activities than anyone else. I wanted to be a part of things. It never dawned on me that there wouldn't be enough hours in the day to do everything. . . . My mother knew I would not turn down anything.

Their practice of never wasting a moment made the women uncomfortable when they were not actively "on task." One woman spoke of her discomfort when she felt she was wasting time. She was vividly in touch with the notion that "[w]arriors never waste an instant" (281). As she put it:

I want to be accomplishing something. I belong to a stock club, and we meet once a month to invest our stock. As soon as we get that done, I am ready to go. There are those who want to sit around and drink coffee and eat donuts the rest of the day. I think—I've got to get out of here. When you have worked all of your life like I have, even going to the beauty shop and having your hair done—sitting under the dryer—I am thinking—I am wasting my time! I think it goes back to my upbringing, when I do, I find very few times when I was doing only one thing at a time. I remember when I was in college, I had my son sitting in my lap playing with a toy, and I was studying. While my husband, on the other hand, if he was studying, he was studying. Everyone else had to be away from him.

THINKING ABOUT MORE THAN ONE THING AT A TIME

Another thing that the women in the study did to compress time was to think about more than one thing at a time, to make connections between and among things that generally were overlooked. Making the connections helped them see how two or three things could happen in concert, or how the activities of one project served multiple projects. The multiple projects or issues, then, became smaller components of a larger activity or issue.

One woman, for example, talked about how the demands of the job made her categorize all her activities as ultimately the same activity and to discard everything else that was unnecessary. She was able to intuitively see a deeper level of similarities in issues that she faced. This helped her to compress tasks and discard anything superficial or trivial.

I have found that my world has become reduced to very few intersections in a very narrow channel in a very limited world view as superintendent. All of the intersections have different names—the groups, the committees, the problems, the task, the whatever. They're all different issues superficially, but at a deeper level, they are all the same—they are all the same because you are moving to completion of the problem in all of them.

It is important to understand that grasping connections between and among things is grasping reality. Further, grasping these connections quickly compresses time.

I am not a physicist, but have read some of the literature for lay people focused on quantum physics, systems theory, biology, and chaos theory (Capra 1975, 1982, 1996; Gleick 1987, Wheatley 1992). This literature reveals that these connections are deep, profound, and physical. As Wheatley (1992) writes, "Day after day, as we inhale and exhale, we give off what were our cells, and take in elements from other organisms to create new cells" (103).

The knowledge that scientists have gained from their newfound acquaintance with the subatomic level is surprisingly reminiscent of the ancient knowledge and wisdom of many cultures. Native Americans, for example, have used language that gives us distinct impressions that they had and have an awareness of the subatomic level of matter. Consider a quote from Ted Perry that was inspired by Chief Seattle (quoted in Capra 1996);

> This we know.
> All things are connected
> like the blood
> which unites one family. . . .
>
> Whatever befalls the earth,
> befalls the sons and daughters of the earth.
> Man did not weave the web of life;
> he is merely a strand in it.
> Whatever he does to the web,
> he does to himself. (xi)

Castaneda's writings about Yaqui Indians of Northern Mexico also reflect the deep connections between and among things. In my view, that is why the Principles of Power that Castaneda suggests were used to train warriors are tremendously helpful when expressing elements of leadership that are often overlooked in literature based on the mechanical model of Newtonian physics. Contemporary thought has shifted from the mechanical model to an organic biological/ecological model. Certainly, discussion of time/space is one that brings to the table a need to move from the mechanical model to a model that reflects the connections in systems and includes the fullest description of connection in environments.

The discussion about thinking and connections takes us further into these new understandings of matter and energy.

VIEWING THE ROLE AS ONE RELATIONAL THING TO DO

Perhaps one of the most important connections that the women in the study made was achieved when they were able to see everything they did as one connected, comprehensive whole. This view of their work came about because they had one primary focus—caring relationships with adults and children. (See chapters 4 and 6 for the full discussion.) The development and support of caring relationships was the foundation of their work.

Relationships take time. But if a role is perceived to be about relationships then questions about how and what should be done can be answered with consistency. This is not to say that quality has to suffer or should suffer when relationship is foundational to work. Indeed, when viewing relationships as the connection between and among everyone, it can be understood that lack of quality affects everyone—it is not an isolated event or characteristic. The superintendents in the study had conversations with others in the culture to express that one person's shame created shame for the entire system. They emphasized that all people were responsible for and to each other. This was not part of public relations rhetoric. In fact, they quickly and openly admitted mistakes that had been made in the district or in their own practice.

And yet, they remained focused on positive caring relationships. Some of the other women in the study recalled instances when they took the extra time to support people in their districts. One superintendent recalled:

> I pay attention to people's feelings. I just had an experience the other day when I was in the middle of one of the principal's goal-setting meetings. I spend an hour with each principal. The principal, with whom I was working, was extremely stressed out. She is a fine person, I've known her for years. I could see that she was stressed out. She started the meeting by saying, "I'm going to take a leave of absence." And the next thing I knew, she was in tears. I said, "Just relax, take a deep breath, let's think."
>
> After our meeting, she told another one of the principals—who told me this today—that she felt like a new person when she left. She said, "That [superintendent] really paid attention." She had two big issues that she was dealing with. I picked up the phone and helped get them fixed. I got her the support that she needed to get a couple of things worked out with two families and so forth. I think that women [when they are superintendents] pay attention to these things. I could tell that she was stressed.

Clearly, as established in other chapters, relationships were very important to the women in the study. Without a doubt, relationship development requires a lot of time.

Interestingly, feminist literature suggests that such relationship development is critical for all educational leaders. As Margaret Grogan (1998) states: "In the end, educational leaders who attempt to operate in the absence of relationships will find themselves alone, unable to provide a connected environment in which children learn and prosper" (28). This literature draws attention to the fact that connections made between people and children in educational and community settings directly affect the well-being academically[1] and personally of children.

Relationship building was also a part of the decision-making processes in the districts of the women superintendents in the study. (For full discussion, see chapter 11.) Anyone who has tried to work with others during collaborative decision-making processes is aware of their time-intensive nature. Diana Pounder (1998), in her book, *Restructuring schools for collaboration: Promises and pitfalls*, wrote about the costs associated with increased collaboration. She stated, "These costs include increased time and effort associated with joint planning, communication, coordination, and monitoring of complex collaborative programs and processes" (176).

And while these findings cannot be minimized, the superintendents in the study didn't view this way of spending time as an increase in time spent. This type of decision making was *the* way they made decisions. And they made them this way, in large part, because such processes are relational in nature. They also understood that they had a choice. One, they could make decisions quickly without the input of many and spend time later correcting the mistakes they made, or two, they could take the time with people during the decision-making process and have fewer poor or faulty decisions. They chose to spend time in relationships with people, so the second option, collaborative decision making, was a natural choice.

One administrator in one of the districts talked about the superintendent's (one of the participants) decision-making process,

> I guess the best way I could describe it [her decision-making process] is as a participatory style of management. She involves a lot of people in decision making. To the point where a decision really may not be even classified as her own, but it's classified as a group decision.

All of the women in the study used collaborative decision-making processes in their work. They did not hesitate because of time requirements. Their valuing of other people was at the core of this type of decision making and to do otherwise would have been to move against their own hearts.

Understanding Patterns of Uncertainty and Ambiguity

For the superintendents in the study, changing plans became necessary when anything of more importance needed to be prioritized over other planned events. Thus, ambiguity was a part of their schedules. Nothing on the calendar was an absolute certainty.

I remember being poised to observe meetings, even large meetings, that were postponed or cancelled thirty minutes before they began. Whole days shifted as a result. And these changes became a normal part of the culture—something not easily accepted by the culture especially in the beginning. The words "living with ambiguity"—touted by most leadership experts as a requirement of leadership and organizations of the future (Bennis 1989; Hesselbein, Goldsmith, and Beckhard 1996; Morgan 1993; Wheatley 1992)—were a part of the women superintendents' rhetoric and professional practices.

"Walking the talk" of living with ambiguity was not easy. The traditional attitudes toward time—starting on time, finishing on time, not wasting time, respecting time—often hung heavily in the atmosphere. People in these districts had concerns that the culture would look disorganized—because of the traditional ways that outsiders viewed organizations. They knew that other things were gained, however. For one thing, not only the superintendent, but also others in the system became much more responsive to internal and external needs.

For example, one day while in the middle of a meeting in the largest urban district in the sample, a memo was handed to the superintendent. The memo communicated that a student had been murdered across the street from the campus at one of the middle schools (2,000 students) right before school began. In a district that large, it would have been acceptable for officials other than the superintendent to immediately respond to the news. The superintendent could have followed later.

That is not what happened. Instead, the superintendent stopped the meeting and went straight to the site, making calls on her mobile phone on the way. I rode along and watched her work all day at the school to support the principals and teachers as they located the student with the gun (who was still in the building), held other students in their classrooms during the search, listened to witnesses, worked with the police, communicated with parents, the press, and of course all of the students, faculty, and staff.

As the morning progressed, the superintendent reviewed announcements and press releases with the principals, police, counsellors, and other experts, guiding and actually helping the emotionally distraught principals and teachers think through what they were going to do. She never took over, but constantly asked questions and helped guide and synthesize the ideas that came from the group of people who worked to get through the school day and still keep the rest of the school population safe and feeling somewhat secure. At the end of that first day, she and others addressed the whole faculty and staff in one of the most moving gatherings of my life.

Her work with all of the players in the drama of that day was that of an important team member who belonged to what became a very able team. And, during the rest of that week and the months that followed, she remained an active part of the school's process of recovery. I cannot overstate the importance of her presence in terms of the success of others in this most difficult of situations. If she had been rigid in her approach to time, she would not have acted as quickly and naturally in response to the situation. She definitively knew what her schedule needed to become— she prioritized her work with students, teachers, administrators, and parents. Safety, care, and thoughtful comprehensive action determined the pace of her day rather than a concern for efficiency and certainty. She lived with ambiguity during this tragedy and during every other day of her life.

The fact that the women in the study overtly displayed an ability to live with uncertainty and ambiguity was evidence to me that they intuitively understood aspects of order that exist within apparent disorder. They also talked in ways that made it apparent that they understood time differently than most people. Consider the language of one of the women in the study when she said,

> There are so many decisions that have to be made. It isn't like one decision is going to be made and everything else stops. And then you go on to another decision and everything stops. Everything happens at once. Everything happens in parallel. Everything happens at the same time, and there's no pausing. One process doesn't pause so you can fully realize another process.

In this statement, the woman has compressed all of the decisions that had to be made into one event. They all happen at the same time. Out of disorder—all these decision-making processes going on without pauses—came the ultimate order. They all happen at the same time without pause. All the micro events become one macro event. As Ludwig Boltzmann might put it, as the number of possible complexions increases, and with it the degree of disorder, there results a new order (Capra 1996, 186). To make this concept clearer to the reader, I turn to an example from Capra (1996) that provides a visual.

> Suppose we fill a bag with two kinds of sand, the bottom half with black sand and the top half with white sand. This is a state of high order; there is only one possible complexion [other arrangement—the black sand could be on top and the white sand could be on the bottom]. Then we shake the bag to mix up the grains of sand. As the white and the black sand get mixed more and more, the number of possible complexions increases, and with it the degree of disorder, until we arrive at an equal mixture in which the sand is of a uniform gray and there is maximum disorder. (187)

Capra continues to explain that maximum disorder is a new order. What was once two distinct parts, after moving through stages of increasing disorder, became only one orderly whole. It was neither black nor white, instead it was gray. But, as a single unit it was more orderly than any other configuration. The one thing that is misleading about the example, however, is the erroneous conclusion that once the sand is completely mixed, it is in a stable state. Actually, at the subatomic level, the molecules never stop moving. So, there is a constant move through states that feel like order and disorder. This constant change is what creates uncertainty and, thus, ambiguity, in life as we experience it.

The women superintendents in the study had a surprising intuitive understanding of these concepts. I don't mean that they talked about these things in the way Capra, Gleick, and Wheatley do, but they did use the language of uncertainty and ambiguity. And, they talked about how all things were interconnected in ways that created one "sort of" amalgamated thing. Further, they appeared to understand through their experiences as superintendents that the interconnections between and among things allowed those things to be compressed—thus producing an effect that could be described as "compressed time."

TIME LEADERS

Perhaps the ability of the women in the study to compress time puts them in positions of being time leaders rather than time managers. Grasping interconnections means that people can deal with multiple intersecting realities rather than one reality at a time. Such an ability compresses time.

Carlos Castaneda (1981) expresses some of these ideas by saying that warriors "turn their heads" not to face a new direction, "but to face time in a different way. [Warriors] face the oncoming time. Normally we face time as it recedes from us. Only [warriors] can change that and face time as it advances on them" (294). One thing that this statement reminds me of is the nonlinear nature of time.

It is only when time recedes from us that we can organize it in a linear way. As we work to plan the future and the events of our days, we pretend that we are shaping the future in a linear fashion. Then, as we pass through our days and nights, little happens in the same way it looked on our planning calendars. But once it is over, we make decisions about what is to be remembered ,and what is to be forgotten. We shape a linear history out of what we have experienced by discounting a lot of it.

It is this same view of time as linear that has defined the word *eternity*. And, when Castaneda speaks of the "second [that] is an eternity," we make the mistake of thinking that somehow that second becomes longer. As Raines (1973) suggests, "We confuse duration with significance—as I was reminded recently at the funeral of the sixteen-year-old boy. The significance of his life is not to be measured in terms of its length, but in terms of the depth of his every day, the fullness, the totality, the wild, open abandon with which he gave himself, day by day, to his days" (83). It is the significance of each moment that defines eternity, for "eternity is not linear . . . is not permanence, but significance; not duration, but depth" (Raines 1973, 83).

Mistakenly, we have come to believe that we can control time and our lives by parcelling them out in hours and minutes. It is when we finally give up this illusion that we can turn and face time as it advances, letting it slide over and around us like the wind—something that we can harness for power, that we can even feel in our hair, but something that we can never see.

WHY MUST SUPERINTENDENTS BE TIME LEADERS
INSTEAD OF TIME MANAGERS?

This chapter began with the ways that the women superintendents in the study understood and thought about time. This section asks the somewhat obvious question: Why is this new understanding of time so critical for all superintendents, and in particular, for women superintendents?

In this section, first I explore the additional time demands in the lives and professional practices of the women in the study that are unique because of gender. These gender-related time demands escalate the time crisis for women superintendents. Following that discussion is a brief overview and critique of what some of the superintendency literature has to report and to advise about time management. The chapter ends with the voices of the Assembly.

THE TIME CRISIS

To begin, superintendents have work days that average twelve hours and work weeks that average from sixty to seventy hours (Norton, Webb, Dlugosh, and Sybouts 1996). Clearly, time is an issue for people in the position. Hughes Chapman (1997) retells a first-year superintendent's description of her work day: "When I ran out of time during the regular day on my calendar, then I started meeting people for lunch and meeting people for dinner. I've been getting home at 9 or 9:30 every evening, and my planning time is being usurped. I know this can be deadly; it can be a deadly mistake" (11).

The time demands on superintendents are known to be extreme to anyone familiar with the role. For women, time demands are even more extreme. This section first discusses two reasons that demands are greater for women.

WOMEN AND THE TIME DEMANDS OF THE SUPERINTENDENCY

The study made clear that the women superintendents had the same demands on their time that all superintendents experience. They all put in an average of seventy to eighty hour weeks. I came to understand, however, that there were at least two major additional time demands placed on the women—because of gender—that were not required of men in the same position: 1) Women in a male role were expected to do not only what men do, but also what women traditionally do in the workplace; 2) The women in the study still had the majority of home responsibilities in addition to their jobs as superintendents.

Taking Time for Gender Expectations in the Role Just knowing that there were two sets of expectations for women superintendents was not enough. To be successful in the role, the women had to address expectations with action. When the two sets of expectations conflicted, the women had to blend and/or balance them, as is evident in the other chapters. (See chapter 5 for the full discussion.)

Time Demands of the Home After the time demands of the workday schedule and the time demands of meeting both role- and gender-related expectations, household and family demands are significant. Consider the data from a 1996 report: married and single men spend about 1.8 hours per day on household and family tasks, employed married women spent much more time on household tasks and family tasks than employed single women do (4.6 hours per day to 3.5 hours); and, employed single women spend more than twice as much time on household and family tasks as single men (Robinson and Converse 1966). Therefore, regardless of employment outside the home, women continued to spend a large amount of time on these tasks when compared to working men.

So, for women, homelife and family—married or single—still means more work than it does for men. As Gupton (1998) stated,

> Although gender equity in the workplace still has a way to go across all professions, the gains women have made toward equitable treatment in the workplace have not been paralleled in the home. Society's persistent sex role-biases today may still put women at a disadvantage in competing for jobs and benefits in the workplace, but people are far more willing for women to share the traditional male role of breadwinner than they are for men to assume shared responsibilities in the traditional housewife's role. . . . CNN Headline News recently reported the results of a current study on stress that further corroborates women's dilemma in balancing home and work responsibilities. The study focused on stress and its effects on working men and women. Working women with children in the home experienced the highest levels of stress, while males with children in the home showed no more stress than the males with no children at home (July 23, 1997). This is consistent with research that repeatedly shows that males, unlike working females, seldom mention family and home responsibilities as significant deterrents to their work or sources of stress. (182)

One of the women in the study talked about the workload she faced at home. She told me that she worked at home and the office. She felt that she was "on duty" at home and at work, and that her husband believed that he was "on duty" at work and "off duty" at home. She commented that she didn't have a place where she was "off duty." She talked about her role at home:

> I am not married to someone who sees his role as taking over the household piece or the child care piece just because I have a job as a superintendent. I mean his job is equally demanding. He's not happy when I am wearing too many hats because in his mind I'm not doing what I should be doing. He never cooks. He wouldn't know how to cook. I still do that. And I

still do a lot of those house pieces. And it's an expectation
from family. And from time to time, I think about that. But, I
do know one thing. I think he [her husband] recognized early
on that I have to do certain things, or I wouldn't be happy.
And I think he's just sort of accepted that as what comes with
the territory [being married to her].

ADVICE ABOUT TIME MANAGEMENT FROM THE LITERATURE

Clearly, time demands are constant for women superintendents and coping
with the relentlessness of these demands is physically, intellectually, spiritually, and emotionally draining. Norton et al. (1996) offer advice to
superintendents:

> There is not time for energy lapses, and so the superintendent
> should set aside some time each day for exercise, sensible
> food, and time to reflect on the events of the day and week.
> School leaders must be aware of situations that cause stress
> and learn to deal with them in appropriate, effective ways. . . .
> Finally, it is important to establish an agenda that allows for
> reading about current trends in education, research in curricu-
> lum, instruction, and leadership, and activities of state and
> federal officials. (65)

While it may be good advice, such counsel adds more demands to the
superintendent's day and takes even more time from the superintendent's schedule. What a dilemma! In order to handle the time-consuming
demands of the superintendency, a person must give up more time in
order to stay healthy enough to meet the demands.

Konnert and Augenstein (1990) take a little different approach. They
open with a comment about the time requirements of all administrators.
They distinguish between building-level administrators and superintendents by saying that the superintendent is the only one in the school district who has almost complete control over personal time allocation. They
continue, "The superintendent can determine which issues are worthy of
personal attention, and those that will be delegated. The superintendent
should be able to do a better job of planning personal time allocation
than the building administrators, because the superintendency is more
isolated from the minute-to-minute operation of the school day than the
principalship" (55).

And with another interesting twist they continue, "The superintendent also influences the way the other administrators within the system
spend their time. This is done by direct request and by constantly com-

municating with them on what is important in the system" (55). They end their discussion by asserting that the superintendent has more responsibility than other administrators to spend time thinking. They suggest that the superintendent is paid to be "creative and innovative in idea generation and problem solving" (55).

Thus, the literature, if it discusses time at all, establishes—with empirical evidence—that the superintendents' job comes with impossible time demands, but the literature also suggests that the superintendent has more control over time allocation than other administrators. The sum total of the advice in the literature is very confusing.

1) The superintendent's job demands on average from sixty to seventy hours a week—usually more than any other job in the district.

2) In order to manage the tremendous energy drain of a job that takes so much time, more time must be taken for staying healthy enough to give the amount of energy required.

3) Superintendents have more control over their use of time because they can delegate work and set their own calendars more often than other administrators.

4) Since superintendents have more control over their time than other administrators, it is their responsibility to influence the way other administrators spend their time.

5) Superintendents must allocate more of their time to thinking than any other administrator because they are supposed to be innovative and creative in idea generation and problem resolution—another time requirement.

There is little said in the literature about time that is helpful. And it certainly does not discuss or give advice about how to handle the additional time demands of "work at home." To say that the superintendency is a twenty-four-hour job—as is often reported in the literature—doesn't catch it for women who are still doing the majority of the work at home. Somehow, their days need to contain more than twenty-four hours. And, the only way that the women in the study could get more out of a twenty-four hour day, was to compress time—as described in the first part of this chapter.

THE ASSEMBLY

The Assembly had a lot to say about Principle Six. A few felt strongly that women approach work differently than men, especially when it comes to time and activity. Perhaps if they had been given the words, they might have said that some women face time in a different way than some men. One superintendent recalled:

> I just recently had a conversation with colleagues—both men and women—about how females tend to be doing at least two things at once. They're sitting in a meeting and listening, but they are also making an agenda for something else. The men tend to be focused on one issue at a time. And sometimes, the men interpret that the women aren't listening. One of the men superintendents in the group said he gets very frustrated because he feels that the women aren't necessarily paying attention to what's going on.

It was clear from her comment that the men in the group thought the women just weren't paying attention. In fact, it irritated some of the men. They couldn't imagine that the women were doing two things at once, when in truth they were.

Another superintendent joined in:

> I can relate to what you are saying. Yes, we have all these little tasks that we are responsible for that need to get done and nothing ever comes to a closure point—and yes, put in a load of laundry in while you are at it, too. We're trying to get so much into the eighteen-hour days so we push it together—compress it. Males don't seem to be able to do that. They tend to take a task and carry it to completion. And maybe start a second task but they don't get deeply into that second task. Then when the first task is done they go to the next task. It's kind of like cutting the grass and then trimming. I carry the trimmer with me as I'm cutting the grass. (Laughing) I don't like to go back around and trim.

One of the women who was not a superintendent had another view. She suggested,

> Since I'm not a superintendent, I may not know what I'm talking about, but it seems to me that both men and women superintendents are doing eighteen things at once. What I think is different for women is that women also have to take care of families. They have even more to juggle than the men. Maybe if you can't handle multiple tasks at one time, you aren't cut out for the position. You won't last, you won't survive, and you won't enjoy it. So while men have a lot going on too, they don't have to worry about whether or not the kid has to go to the dentist or whether or not the laundry is done.

> There is a whole other set of tasks that live in the minds of women along with the job set. Men have spouses to take care of these things. Even at conferences there is an effort to appreciate the spouses who support their husbands so they can do the time-consuming job of the superintendency.

Another woman brought up an interesting point:

> Well, I wonder what those women who are spouses, and who make baskets or whatever at conferences—I wonder what they do in their real lives. We know that a lot of those women have their own jobs too. They have to be something besides simply being the support to their husbands. So, they are not only making wicker baskets at conferences but maybe holding responsible positions which also have outside demands on them. Who's picking up the pieces for them? Who's helping them with their work?

This comment hit home for the Assembly. It nailed us in a certain way. As women, we buy into the idea that women need to be a support system so that men can do their work with no other responsibilities. And yet, working women—including us—certainly don't receive the same treatment from the men in their lives (as was discussed under the section on "Time Demands on Women Superintendents" in this chapter).

Further, think about the women administrators' conferences. There are no activities for spouses at those conferences. Husbands and partners rarely come with their working wives, nor do they take part in planned activities such as woodcrafts or whatever. So, while we know all of this, we continue to applaud women (spouses) who do these things for their husbands and partners, and somehow we believe that our applause recognizes what the women are doing in a positive sense—and in some ways it does.

However, we rarely think about how our applause reifies a system that treats men as if they are superior to women. We forget that those very women whom we applaud are many times expected to donate their time and energy unfairly to a household, just as we do. We, by our applause, are idealizing their role and making it even more difficult for them and, indeed for us, to insist on equality in our public and privates lives. We also forget that the job of the superintendency would be much more doable if it wasn't constructed in a way that so heavily relied on, literally, a wife to pick up all of the pieces. If the job had been constructed for just one person rather than two, all superintendents would be happier and by far healthier.

One of the women superintendents picked up on this notion and stated:

> I think that the decline of partners programs even for super-intendents' conferences is an indicator that more and more women are working and not able to be that superintendent's wife of the past. Time for the job will become more of a factor, because wives are working, so men will not get the same support when they are superintendents.

This topic led into a discussion of what support systems looked like—how they too have a particular cultural description, and how if a person doesn't have the right looking support system they are pretty much left to fend for themselves. They are "outsiders."

The Assembly then returned to the issue of time and the demands of the superintendency. One woman offered:

> I do think that the superintendency is a twenty-four-hour job. And that most communities expect you—regardless of gender—to be on call and live in a glass house. And people do pay atten-tion to what you buy at the grocery store and talk to you every-where you are and they want you to be there in the community. That is the nature of the job. In a way, the job is a mission. You are committing your life to it. And I think that is dif-ferent than a lot of other jobs or careers. But I think there are significant benefits because you do have, I think a real satis-faction of thinking and believing and influencing the direction of education. And that is at least the satisfaction that I get from it. And it's enough satisfaction that keeps me coming back each day—that allows me to commit twenty-four hours a day to such a thing.

The comments made next by another one of the superintendents was evidence that the role of superintendent is changing. And time spent on the job is beginning to look different in some districts. As she said,

> Even within the position, I think there is great room for difference. I could never, ever be in a position where I was under the watchful eye of people twenty-four hours a day. And yet, I know that the description was how things usually are for superintendents. Yet, I could not be that kind of super-intendent. I wouldn't be happy. I wouldn't be successful. I wouldn't be there long, by my own choice.
>
> Still, I'm finishing my seventh year as a superintendent, and most days I wouldn't trade it for any other job in the world. But I tend to be much more independent, much more reserved, much more my own person. I don't live in the com-

munity. I like to eat dinner with my husband without people stopping off to talk to me. I don't like going to the grocery store and talking to everybody there when I'm you know, picking my words. I like some anonymity. Even though I love being with people, I like arm's length from them, too. I want balance in my life. I need a balance between my personal life and my professional lives that keeps both of them very closely connected but in a very special way that's right for me.

This superintendent's discussion of the connection and at the same time the distance between her personal and professional lives recognized her ability to see the varying complexions that were present as the two mixed. Her solution to these multiple complexions, which could appear chaotic to many people, was to keep the professional and personal balanced with each other. Such an arrangement kept the black sand and the white sand (recall this example from earlier) mixed in a way that she had one life—one life that was a composite mixture of the two. She understood that without balanced amounts of each, the mixture became chaotic. And, yet, when balance was established her whole life had a more consistent feel to it. Both aspects of her life were attended to as one life, rather than thinking of them as two separate lists of tasks and activities. In this way, she compressed time.

Another superintendent talked about how she compressed time when she said:

> I compress time by flashing forward in time and bringing what I see in that future place to bear on what I am currently doing. We may have to get bloody here in order to win the battle down there.

Still another woman talked about time compression as a type of metacognition, an activity in which she was aware of her many layers of thought and she caught herself in them. When that happened the layers could affect each other and change each other in ways that could not happen when thoughts were laid out in a linear fashion.

Later in the discussion, one of the women talked about the part of the principle that states, "In battle for your life, a second is an eternity; an eternity that may decide the outcome" (281).

> I think that when we are making decisions about the lives of children, that is the battle of our lives. So, when we are in a difficult situation, and we have one second to decide how we are going to react, our perceptions make a huge, huge difference in the eventual outcomes. So, those things I value most—how

I perceive—become the driving force behind my "one second" decisions. I'm going to do everything I can to be collaborative, to be above board, to be positive, to think of children. Because indeed, that acting out of my perceptions becomes a part of the reality of how people experience an event, and that lasts for an eternity and determines what happens next.

This woman understood that eternity is not linear or duration, rather it is significance. Clearly, the women of the Assembly saw the depth of meaning in Castaneda's Sixth Principle.

CHAPTER 11

PRINCIPLE SEVEN

EXERCISING POWER

A [warrior] never pushes him[her]self to the front.

—Carlos Castaneda, *The Eagle's Gift*

Power and the exercise of power is at the heart of a warrior's social role in Castaneda's world, and at the heart of the school superintendent's social role in our world. Castaneda's trainer was most impressed with Principle Seven, teaching Carolos that in order to apply the seventh principle, one has to apply the other six. Interestingly, a good portion of the narratives from the women in the study centered on this principle, thus, making it the most important principle in the data gathered.

For the superintendents in the study, pushing themselves to the front meant wielding power. And that is in itself a complex issue for women in a traditional position of power. Thus, to begin, a brief history of the concept of power is appropriate.

THEORETICAL CONCEPTIONS OF POWER

Theoretical analyses of the concept of power generally occur along two primary trajectories (Clegg 1989, 21–38; Hartsock 1981, 3–19; Pitkin 1972, 276–277; Stone 1989, 219–233; Wartenberg 1990, 9–50). The dominant trajectory in the history of political thought and in contemporary political science defines power as control, command, domination over others—as "power over" (Clegg 1989; Hartsock 1981). The subordinate (less emphasized, analyzed, and appreciated) trajectory defines power as a capacity to accomplish certain social goals through cooperation among agents with various interests and concerns—as "power with/to" (Follett 1942; Sarason 1990).

This chapter includes a brief review of the scholarly literature on the concept of power to make three points: 1) The discussion of power has been excessively narrow; 2) Female theorists have been more likely than male theorists to emphasize the collaborative conception of power; 3) Although not obvious on the surface, traditional gender roles in the United States have predisposed women toward "power with/to" and have drawn men to social roles which expect them to exercise "power over." In this chapter, we can see that women superintendents in this study have emphasized "power with/to" in their work lives, creating a natural practice of "not pushing themselves to the front" as Principle Seven insists.

POWER OVER

According to John Stuart Mill (1869, 208), "A man's power is the readiness of other men to obey him." It would be convenient to assert that this quotation sums up a long lineage of male political philosophers discussing power as a male property in terms that are exclusively competitive, controlling, commanding. As Wartenberg (1990), Clegg (1989), Hartsock (1981), and others have shown, however, great works in the history of political thought cannot be so simply read. It is more accurate to assert that contemporary political scientists and sociologists have largely conceived and analyzed power as command, control, and domination.

The dominant trajectory of power research in this century emerged from the work of Max Weber (1924), who defined power as the imposition of one's will upon the behavior of others, and who regarded domination by authorities and obedience by subordinates as important requisites to social action and bureaucratic performance.

Bertrand Russell (1938), Harold Lasswell and Abraham Kaplan (1950), and Herbert Simon (1953) each contributed to the "power over" paradigm of power by seeking to define power in operational terms that facilitated scientific analysis of the concept. By defining power as a change in the behavior of an actor, produced by another agent, Simon not only distinguished power from such resources as wealth and status—which might contribute to it—but he provided a definition of power that, at least in principle, permitted its direct measurement. Such an understanding of power became central to the theory of pluralism, the orthodox model of political power structures in political science at the height of the behavioral revolution. Robert Dahl (1961), Jack Nagel (1975), and Nelson Polsby (1980) each insisted that power could be detected, measured, and analyzed only by measuring the policy preferences of various actors and the actual outcomes of concrete political decisions. The existence of a dominant group, a power elite, could be demonstrated only by showing that elites consistently got what they wanted in the policy process while the resulting policies consistently ran counter to the preferences of other (subordinate) groups. According to pluralist analyses, "power over" was widely exercised in various political communities and indeed was central to all political processes, but power elites were difficult to discern in the fragmented power structures of America.

While radical political analysts disputed this conclusion and the methods of pluralists, they continued to conceive of power as domination and control. According to Bachrach and Baratz (1962), pluralists examined only one "face" of power: the power that was exercised after issue agendas and policy preferences were set. They suggested that "power over" or controlling power was much more extensive and concentrated than was suggested by observing the broad participation of various groups and interests in policy formulation. A second face of "power over" was discernible in the capacity of a small number of elites to control the agenda of American politics by preventing issues that could generate radical change from receiving serious consideration. A third face of "power over" was also discernible in the ideological hegemony that powerful interests had over the general public. By influencing what people wanted—by getting people to want outcomes that departed from their true needs and instead conformed to what the elite wanted them to want—elites could exercise a rather hidden but highly pervasive form of domination (Lukes 1974, Schumaker 1991).

Beyond the three faces of "power over," a number of male theorists have also sought to conceptualize other forms of domination. During the 1970s, Michel Foucault defined power as a mechanism that excludes, rejects, denies, obstructs, and obfuscates; for Foucault (1977), this "disciplinary power," which he uncovered in various "disciplines"—medicine, psychiatry, penology, criminology, and the various social sciences—transformed human beings into subjects, persuading humans to participate in their own subjugation (Ball 1993, 27–28). In his early writings, Clarence Stone (1980) discussed "systemic power" as durable features of social, economic, and political systems that consistently advantage some groups while disadvantaging others. Such innovative conceptions of power moved away from the behavioral approaches that measured how individuals were controlled and instead embraced approaches that are more structural, that focus on the controlling properties of social systems writ large. But these conceptions continued along the "power over" trajectory that has dominated political science and sociology even up to the present day (Hartsock 1987).

POWER WITH/TO

While (mostly) male political theorists and scientists were proposing and analyzing these various aspects of "power over," and while they were debating among themselves the scientific viability of these conceptions of power, the most prominent female political theorist of the twentieth century, Hannah Arendt, sought to reestablish the trajectory of power that had been largely abandoned by contemporary analysts. According to Arendt (1972, 143), "Power corresponds to the human ability not just to act but to act in concert. Power is never the property of an individual; it belongs to a group and remains in existence only so long as the group keeps together."

Arendt was concerned that politics had degenerated into a mere power struggle, characterized by the use of strength, force, and violence. For Arendt, politics was more than a matter of domination; it was or could be a process by which free and equal agents create collective power, the capacity to act in concert to achieve collectively those common goals that individuals cannot achieve for themselves. Politics thus involves acts of persuasion, communication, and cooperation that establish collaborative relationships among people and that enable transformations of problematic social conditions. Power, then, is a capacity that a community of people attain when their acts of communication, cooperation, and collaboration have been successful (see Wartenberg 1990, 33–50, and Ball 1993, 20–25).

Arendt's approach to the concept of power was emphasized and elaborated by Nancy Hartsock (1981, 1983), who clearly differentiated a masculine emphasis on power as domination from an alternative feminine tradition. According to Hartsock (1983, 210),

> [T]heories of power put forward by women rather than men
> differ systematically from the understanding of power as domi-
> nation. While few women have theorized about power, their
> theories bear a striking similarity both to one another and to

theories of power recently characterized as feminist understandings of power. My several cases clearly constitute only
suggestive evidence for my argument. Yet I believe it is significant that I was unable to discover any woman writing about
power who did not stress those aspects of power related to
energy, capacity, and potential.

Hartsock did not propose a fixed alternative conception to power as
domination, but found intriguing possibilities in the writings of such
women as Arendt, Dorothy Emmet, and Hannah Pitkin. In Arendt, she
saw a model in which the heroic person finds her power not through
dominating others in competitive situations, but through "action in connection with others with whom one shares a common life and common
concerns" (Hartsock 1983, 217). In Emmet (1953–54), she saw a useful
distinction between coercive power and coactive power, and found a
hopeful attempt to redefine power as "any kind of effectiveness in performance" (Hartsock 1983, 223). In Pitkin (1972, 275), she saw an
attempt to connect power to community and the capacity of the community to act toward common ends.

Nancy Hartsock (1987, 276–277) agrees with other theorists that
the idea of power in "power over" is significantly different than power
defined as "power with/to." But she takes this division further by calling
for a theory of power for women—a theory that begins from the experience and point of view of the dominated. She points out, "Such theories
would give attention not only to the ways women are dominated, but
also to their capacities, abilities, and strengths. . . . [Such] theories would
use these capacities as guides for a potential transformation of power
relationships—that is for the empowerment of women" (158). Women's
need for a transformation in power relationships is implied in Marshall's
(1985) message when she states that "men have been equated with power,
while the power women were perceived to have was largely a reflection
of the power of the man with or for whom they worked. Women did
[do] not have power on their own" (12). Women struggle with this con-
tradiction, particularly while they occupy a position that is viewed as
powerful—such as the superintendency.

In a recent essay on "Women and Power," Jean Baker Miller (1993)
claimed that women have been powerful in ways that are transparent
next to the masculine perspective of power as domination. Women have,
according to Miller, traditionally experienced their power by producing
change and by empowering others through their roles as mothers and
teachers. According to Miller, power is used by women all the time, but

most often they believe it should be used for the benefit of others. A woman's identity demands that her power be regarded as neither destructive nor selfish for fear that she will be abandoned, and thus women are encouraged to use their capacities in collaborative ways that serve the needs of broader communities.

In short, a significant number of women have written about power in a way that distinguishes "power over" from "power with/to," that generally rebukes applications of "power over," and that finds "power with/to" more compatible with the roles and experiences of women. This is not to say that "power with/to" is an exclusively feminist idea and has been ignored by men.[1] The work of Jürgen Habermas (1981), for example, can be seen as an attempt to facilitate collaborative exercises of power (Ball 1993, 24–25). The realist model of power developed principally by Jeffrey Issac (1993) regards power as something that exists in social roles (prior to any behavioral application) and is necessary for coordinated social action; as such this model regards power as more essential to social productivity than social control. Further, the regime model of power developed by Clarence Stone (1989) holds that the increasingly fragmented structure of societies, in which political communities are held together by loose networks of institutional arrangements, make "comprehensive social control impossible." The costs of getting dissident elements of the community to comply with central commands are impossibly great. According to Stone (1989, 227), the contemporary (urban) political regime must use collaborative power.

> In a fragmented world, the issue is how to bring about enough cooperation among disparate community elements to get things done—and to do so in the absence of an overarching command structure or a unifying system of thought.

Each of these men began to reconceptualize power in ways that emphasize its cooperative and collaborative aspects and recognize that the achievement of social power serves the goals of a community and does not simply subordinate some people to the will of others. Thus, the power with/to model is not only a feminist idea that represents the experiences of women; it may also be an increasingly emergent paradigm of power whose development coincides with the continued maturation of democratic processes in increasingly pluralistic and fragmented societies.

I suggest that new understandings of power, significantly influenced by feminist theory, are beginning to gain prominence in political science and other disciplines concerned with the application of political power.

While feminist theorists on the idea of justice believe that an ethic of care must complement principles of human rights, feminist theorists on the idea of power believe that analyses of power as "collaborative, sharing with others" must complement analyses of power as "social domination" (Stone 1989, 219–233). In other words, feminists view orthodox conceptions of power as incorporating masculine preoccupations with how people control one another to secure their personal wants. They suggest that such conceptions must be complemented with more feminine concerns about how people can effectively organize themselves to solve social problems and transform their environments.

THE WOMEN SUPERINTENDENTS AND POWER

I believe that the collaborative model of power is appropriate for the pluralistic and fragmented cultures found in schools. Further, I assert that the power with/to model—potentially a model able to honor and value collective efforts involving all people—is an essential element in any caring school culture led by a superintendent wishing to address, at least in part, the "pain of all sorts" (Noddings 1984, 1) in today's world. I believe that "action in connection with others with whom one shares a common life and common concerns" (Hartsock 1983, 217) is made possible by those who, in Castaneda's system, are capable of "not pushing oneself to the front."

To be sure, Cantor and Bernay (1992) asserted that unconscious practices and social norms support the perception that power is masculine. In other words, power normatively means asserting a dominate ego or pushing oneself forward—a practice that is in direct opposition to the Seventh Principle.

The women in this study, however, did not practice or define power as social norms dictate or as dominance, authority, or power over others. In fact, they confirmed my earlier research (Brunner 1995) which revealed that "[w]omen who attain positions of power are most successful when they practice female approaches to power which stress collaboration, inclusion, and consensus-building—models based on the belief that one person is not more powerful than another" (24). In collaboration the ego is not pushed forward. It is subordinated to the wider purposes of the collaborative group. This was the case with all the women superintendents whose practices are included in this study. They worked using a collaborative, inclusive consensus-building model. They worked in concert with others rather than in authority or dominance over others. One woman talked about her approach in the following way:

> I bring together the people who will be affected by the decision and say, "Here is the perceived problem. Is this really the problem?" You may find that it is not the real problem, so you come to consensus about what the real problem is. Then you discuss many solutions to come up with a solution which benefits the most people—especially who is affected by it. It needs to be for the greatest good.

This collaborative role was comfortable for her because she did not view herself as powerful in the traditional sense. As one woman put it: "It is difficult for me to say that I have power."

Others of the women also had difficulty when discussing power but were not as clear as the woman above about why they were uncomfortable with the topic. For example, one woman struggled to explain her discomfort:

> I, let's see—I look at power as—how do I look at power? This is interesting because power is not a word that's regularly in my vocabulary.

Raymond's (1986) description of this phenomenon was helpful. She said that "many women tend to regard power ambivalently, as something to be avoided, something that corrupts, and something that is always used over and against others . . . many women having been victims of patriarchal power, have assumed uncritically that power itself corrupts" (as quoted in Adler, Laney, and Packer 1993, 105). Going farther, Jean Baker Miller explained that women are afraid of power because they believe that if they are powerful they will destroy their relationships (see chapters 4, 7, 9). As Cantor and Bernay (1992) expressed it, women also fear that

> they would be acting selfishly if they were to use power [as the dominant culture defines it]. This is because exercising power conflicts with the lifelong messages they have received about devoting their energies to enhance the power of others. Thus, women equate selfishness with destructiveness. They come to fear that such selfishness and destructiveness may result in abandonment by those around them. It is easy to see why women feel threatened by isolation and a loss of their feminine need to serve and connect with others if they were to gather and exert power (in the traditional sense). (52)

Naomi Wolf's (1993) research on women's socialization around the concept of power was also useful in analyzing this phenomenon. At one point she stated:

> Obviously, there is a taboo that make it virtually impossible in "women's language" to directly claim power or achievement. But women's willingness—indeed, their eagerness—to do so when it seems "safe" suggests that this reluctance is not due to women's aversion to asserting their strengths and successes; it is due to women's sense that they are not allowed to assert them. (250)

Women in my study struggled when talking about power. Because it was not "safe" to talk about it in most settings, they didn't have the language to talk about it even in the safety of a private interview. This struggle was especially intense given the fact that they occupied a position that is viewed as powerful—the superintendency. One woman talked about the unsafe or "negative" implications for women related to the notion of power.

> I have a difficult time with the word *power* because it has negative connotations for me. Culturally women were not supposed to be the power base. And their being powerful was not looked upon as a positive characteristic for a female. And so, when you asked me about power, I wanted you to know that I wanted to get around the word. I just want to tell you that as a female, the word just isn't a good word [laughing].

Wolf's (1993) research supports this woman's sense that power is something to be avoided because of influence from not only the dominant male culture, but also from female subcultures. As Wolf asserted,

> [w]omen's claim to power is not held in check only by men; standards set by other women create a strong force that can either inhibit female self-assertion or let it flourish. Women are deeply conditioned to fear visibly "rising above" other women, and their claiming of power is largely determined by how much latitude other women permit them. If the female subculture lets women act like winners, they will; if it punishes that behavior, most will have a much harder time producing it. (250)

Adler, Laney, and Packer's (1993) findings extend Wolf's work. They discovered that women even in less powerful (than the superintendency) positions had difficulty reconciling their role as women with any idea of power. This is evident when they quote a teacher in their study as saying, "I was brought up to be a good little girl. And power doesn't sit easily with that" (95). It is not a grand leap to assume that since most of the child rearing has been done by mothers in our culture, this woman was most strongly influenced by her mother. Accepting this assumption, one could conclude that the woman's mother, as part of a powerful female subculture, taught her daughter that being "feminine" and being powerful do not mix.

Intense discomfort with the term *power* caused some women in the study to find other ways to talk about power in order to avoid the term. One woman said that she was more comfortable using the term *leadership style* rather than the word *power*. When I asked her to define power, she said:

A. I would prefer to talk about leadership style than the use of power.

Q. Why?

A. Probably because that's a more gender-appropriate word. It's okay for me to talk about leadership. It's not always okay for me to talk about power. When I talk about power or act on power, then the negative words start to flow in terms of describing my behavior.

A statement from Wolf (1993) illuminates some of the negative responses this woman identified that caused her to choose the word *leadership* over the word *power*:

> The greatest barriers to women's will to power and leadership were the fear of criticism and the fear of having too much. The women I spoke with described being on the receiving end of criticism as feeling almost physically painful, like a series of blows that left them virtually incapacitated. Many expressed what I too had learned: The punishment they saw as being an inevitable consequence of taking power made the pursuit of leadership or success seem "not worth it." Many saw becoming a leader as dangerous. Paradoxically, they said that the more visibility, recognition, and power they had, the less they felt in control. (251)

The women in the study cautiously searched for ways to talk about power that would ensure their safety. They needed to talk about their work in a way that distanced them from the dominant culture's definition of power. I probed this issue with another woman:

Q. How do you reconcile the fact that you're a woman, and you are in a powerful position and yet the word "powerful" is not comfortable?

A. I think that what you do is you try to play it down.

Deborah Tannen (1994) discussed the effect of downplaying authority. She pointed out that often this action results in a person's being less valued or recognized as accomplished. She suggested that it is possible that when a woman downplays her own authority, she is unintentionally encouraging others to downplay it too or perhaps even to question it (184). "Wearing the mantle of authority lightly," she warned, "allows it to be more easily pushed off your shoulders" (185). This idea was not foreign to the women in my study, and yet it appeared that they had thought through this dilemma in a way that allowed them to "wear the mantle of authority lightly" and still not have it pushed off their shoulders. Consider how the following woman described what she believed to be a change over time in the concept of power in the superintendency. She stated,

> I'm always a little bit surprised when people talk about the power that one holds as a superintendent because it really doesn't seem that their concept of what power has been is part of my definition. In other words, I think people used to talk about an individual being, a superintendent, as being very powerful because what they said was the law—it was passed down, and people had to act and respond to their edict. To me the definition of power is that I have had a part in making something happen that maybe wouldn't have happened without my part in it.

One woman offered her view of power, which demonstrated that for a woman the proper use of power requires that she not push herself forward:

> In a position of power you really are in a position of servant leadership. Your leadership should be to help other people accomplish goals and objectives in the mission in the vision of an organization or a school system, or whatever. I mean that's really what it is to me. Power means assisting other people to accomplish their goals, and that means a lot of collaboration and linking and linkage and bringing people together. That's what power means to me.

Another woman held a very similar view. In fact, this was the view held by all twelve women in the study:

> I define power as the ability to get things done through other
> people. In order to get things done through others you must
> be able to admire the human resources of your staff and build
> personal relationships with highly talented people who want
> to grow, and who want to do their very best. Actually, I never
> think of the superintendency in the sense of power, but if you
> have three things, a talented staff, information and knowl-
> edge, and a network built from personal contacts with people
> with whom you share ideas and information and resources, I
> think you have considerable ability to get things done through
> others and overcome obstacles.

Clearly, this view is one that insists that the superintendent work supportively behind the scenes rather than out in front. One of the women
was explicit about working behind the scenes.

> I'm not particularly comfortable with being recognized as a
> powerful person. I suppose sometimes in some context it
> might be a little bit flattering but I just prefer to stay lower
> key than that. I like to work behind the ranks. I like working
> behind the scenes.

Another characteristic that demonstrated "not pushing oneself to the
front" was seen in the way the women viewed the issue of "getting credit
for one's work." The women in the study, most often, did not care who
got the credit for the work that was accomplished. As one woman stated:

> Nobody may even know that I was involved in an action or
> decision or by the time it all transpires no one will remember
> what it was that catalyzed it. But that's not important. It
> doesn't matter in the least, truly, if anybody else recognizes
> that it started with me.

Another woman said it this way:

> I've always believed that we win when we quit worrying about
> who gets the credit. I want the project complete. If it happens
> by a coalition, then great. I am not interested in claiming that I
> did such and such. I think, as women, we have always known
> that we have to work with people to accomplish anything. A
> mother who runs a household doesn't always get the credit for
> what the children accomplish, but her preparing and planning
> helps these accomplishments to happen.

Still another emphasized that when power was given away, people
became all they could be and deserved credit for their successes.

> I think power is something that you claim when you give it
> away. It is freedom for people to be all that they can be. I
> know that power is very important to some people. Power to
> me is enabling lives to be the very best they can be—to take
> risks to try new and innovative things knowing that they are
> going to be backed if it works and backed if it doesn't work.
> So by enabling your people and improving your people you
> really give yourself a power that comes with watching the
> success of those that you work with.

Perceiving the self as separate from the dominant culture's notion of "power" as "power over" appeared to be necessary for a woman to be truly collaborative. Genuine collaboration occurs when all participants are considered as equals as much as is possible. This attitude and practice, which exemplifies the Seventh Principle, was reflected in some way in all the narratives of the women superintendents.

This is not the whole picture, however. Some of the women reported conflict over the idea of power. For example, you may wonder if these women ever wanted to practice power in the way that our dominant culture defines it—to push themselves forward as an authority or to use power over others.

To be sure, there is a strand of research that suggests that women who seek to influence policy adopt "the strategy of acting like boys" (Schlozman 1990, 375). Certainly, women superintendents seek to influence policy. From this perspective, women attempt to exercise power as dominance in much the same ways that men do. The point is made that they have received the same education about politics as men, because they, too, have been socialized to view politics as competition among competing interests, because selection processes recruit women who accept current ways of thinking about and exercising power, and because women "can only succeed in politics by playing the game as it is currently played" (Verba 1990, 568). A few of them talked about their desires to use power in the way that all of us in this culture have been taught to believe that power is supposed to work, that is, as power over others. One revealed:

> I'm tired of earning power. I'm tired of earning it and creating
> it and collaborating to get it. I'm tired of the informal channels.
> I want a title. I want the salary. I want the responsibility, and
> I want people to expect it from me. I'm way beyond building
> those little vortexes of power in hoping that people will work
> with me. But I would make a sweeping generalization that

> most women don't want power over. In my opinion they want
> the collaborative power model. Very few women are willing
> to do the power over model.

This woman believed that her desire to exert power in a more "masculine" fashion was an unusual one. There is research that suggests that such a move may be necessary at times, however. That research indicates that while women have tried, and continue to try to enter politics using a power with/to or collaborative conception of power (Albrecht and Brewer, 1990), such efforts sometimes fail in an environment in which a conception of power as dominance prevails.

According to Jane Mansbridge (1986), this is one of the major reasons why the women's movement failed to secure passage of the Equal Rights Amendment. Women successfully organized their groups in a way that eschewed the hierarchical power structures that facilitate social control, and adopted communitarian, collaborative, and consensual processes that enabled their groups to get things done internally, within their groups and even within the larger movement. However, these more open and collaborative power arrangements did not often succeed in the state legislatures, where power over conceptions of power continued to dominate the policy process.

Even when faced with the reality that power over movements tend to dominate power with/to efforts, the women superintendents in the study eschewed power used as dominance and control. They were clear that not only did they use power with others because they believed so strongly in maintaining relationships, but also they were severely aware of the negative consequences that they faced if they were confused by their positional power and used power in its traditional—"push to the front"—form. There may be other reasons that the women eschew power used as dominance. Indeed, I have found in research focused on selection of women as superintendents that it is women who define power as with others who appear to have the greatest chance to be selected (Brunner and Schumaker 1998).

And in fact, with the reflection of power as a shared concept in the leadership literature, the women in the study were defining and using power in a way that was congruent with current reform efforts. But I was cautious. I wondered not only about the reasons the women used power as shared, but also about their success in their roles when some literature asserts that the use of this type of power is not effective in policy-setting situations. The success issue was laid to rest quickly when I reviewed the process I used for sample selection (see chapter 2). But I continued to wonder whether the noble self-reports from these women superintendents about the importance of others might be rhetorical and never actually carried out in practice. The triangulation process proved this notion false. When I interviewed people who knew and worked with the women superintendents in the study, I asked them to tell me how their superintendents made decisions and got things done.

- She is less than direct—it is more of a background substance that she possesses that is not confrontational, not frontal.
- She resisted the temptation to take the front position and recognized that the win had to be in a plurality.
- She is a quietly powerful person. She does not wield the power.

Other comments were directly related to the collaborative nature of the women superintendents' decision-making processes.

- She's very much into a team effort.
- Dr. [Name] [when making a decision] will come in with an issue and then people will talk about that backwards, forwards, inside and out. She questions people and they question each other. It's a very open forum.
- [in decision-making] She's not afraid, obviously, to share her ideas and put forth her position, her values, her beliefs about a particular situation, but she does it in such a way that she's not forcing it on people. She's not, and I don't even know how to characterize this, it's not as if the decision had already been made, and she's just simply going through the motions of asking for input and asking for involvement on the part of other people. She truly does seek, accept, and use the ideas and input that people provide to her.

Reports, given during triangulation, about the way the twelve women in my study used power revealed that they stayed in the background as they worked with others, in collaboration, to get things accomplished.

Anne Statham (1987; cited in Tannen 1994) also found that women claimed that their management style was not authoritarian (187). Statham quotes one woman as saying, "I don't care to have that type of attitude . . . you know, crack the whip. I feel more family-oriented to the whole lot of them" (187). Tannen continued by sharing Statham's findings:

> Statham points out that previous studies have divided managers into "task-oriented" and "person-oriented" categories. This dichotomy almost ensures that women will be found

wanting, as any evidence that they are "person-oriented" is then taken to imply they are not "task-oriented," not a very good advertisement when times are hard and companies are concerned with the bottom line—getting the task done. Statham concludes that the women she interviewed were both: They regarded focusing on people as the best way to get the task done. As one female manager put it, "If my people are happy, they are going to do a better job for me—and they do." Statham notes that half the women she interviewed did not describe themselves as people-oriented; it was their secretaries who did. (187)

Statham's findings parallel mine. The women in the study subscribed to the Seventh Principle in a very natural way. By actively pursuing collaboration rather than domination, they did not "push themselves to the front." And just as important, this practice helped them be successful in the role of the superintendency.

THE ASSEMBLY

Perhaps one of the most interesting components of the discussion by the Assembly of the twelve women superintendents' definitions of power and how they used it, was the fact that as superintendents, they were seated in the most powerful position in public school education, and they were uncomfortable with the term *power* defined as dominance, authority, control. The idea that women think about power differently than men, while not broadly discussed, is not new (see for example French 1985; Hartsock 1983; Martinez 1988; Moglen 1983; Raymond 1986; Singer 1987). What was surprising, however, was that when the voices of a good number of women superintendents were heard in concert on the subject, they were talking about power in similar ways—similar to each other, but not similar to the dominant discourse on power.

When I ask people, in general, how they think a superintendent—male or female—would or should define power, they respond that superintendents define power as authority, influence, as "power over." It is difficult to imagine that a person, in the seat of the most powerful, would define it any other way. So, while research on women administrators in less powerful positions shows that they tend to define power as shared or collaborative (see for example Adler, Laney, and Packer 1993; Marshall 1984; Shakeshaft 1989), that research does not look solely at women in the highest position, thus rendering the findings less striking. It is more of a stretch to imagine power practiced as shared when imagining a superintendent of schools. In fact, when thinking about a large urban school district it is almost impossible to imagine power as being used in a collaborative fashion.

However, the Assembly made up of almost all women superintendents, was not surprised. In fact, the group echoed the voices of the twelve women when talking about the dangers that accompanied using power in a dominating, authoritarian way. In no small measure, they could easily recall situations that had caused them difficulty and could attribute their difficulty to a time when they made a decision alone, or had to act in an authoritarian way. Not all of them were as successful in sharing power as a part of their practice as were the twelve women in the study, but it was noted that the twelve women in the study were selected because they were viewed by others to be extremely successful—with "an ability to share power" found to be one of the characteristics that caused a woman to be considered successful in the first place. Thus, the discussion about how they defined and used power was of particular interest to the focus group. They quickly understood the importance of the Seventh Principle, nodding their heads as they individually merged with its meaning.

Some of the most interesting discussion focused on the pitfalls of not following the Seventh Principle. In particular, the women recalled times of difficulty that they believed were directly related to the way they were practicing power at the time. One superintendent stated:

> When I think back about my past experiences, I realize that there have been times when people had difficulty with me. And, as I reflect, I think that what I didn't do was spend time with other people. Somehow I didn't show that I cared about them. I guess I was too task oriented and not enough people oriented. In fact, I always felt uncomfortable in the teacher's lounge when I was a teacher.

A second woman agreed:

> I think that we see aggression as normal behavior for men but abnormal for women. If we [as women] are aggressive, we are out of control.

In general, the Assembly agreed that aggressive behavior "pushed a person to the front," which is a gender-specifically inappropriate "place" for a woman to be. The discussion went farther by probing the deeper meanings of not "pushing oneself to the front." One superintendent told a story:

> One of the principals in the district was sharing with us that he sees the differences in female/male styles. He said that if

you were with a male superintendent he would say, "John, you go get firewood. Ben, you start pitching the tent and so and so, do this." The female superintendent will say, "Who would like to go and gather firewood? Who would like to pitch the tent? Oh, Ben said he would pitch the tent. Is there anyone who would like to help Ben?" So, we as women are natural facilitators. We all laughed at the description of difference between men and women, but it was pretty true in terms of how we as women get people involved in the decision-making process and getting them the information that they need to make and form decisions. And there's that fine line between influence and input.

One woman noted just how important the skill of facilitation was for women so that they weren't too authoritarian. She said,

I think that is an acquired survival skill because if we tell people to go get firewood or anything else, it is viewed differently than when a man does it.

Another superintendent agreed when she added:

And I've seen the trouble that a woman can get into if a female gravitates toward the male style of being directive. The more we as women do that, the more we get into trouble because it creates a clash with how people expect women to behave. And the same thing happens with men if they gravitate toward a female style of consensus building and facilitating. They get into trouble. People tend to reject nontraditional behaviors.

Another superintendent agreed, but brought up another interesting point:

I wonder if another reason we have succeeded is that we are not only great facilitators, but also that we are able to direct when necessary. In fact, that may be what got us the job in the first place. There are times when strong directing capabilities are needed and there are very few of us who don't have the ability to direct.

This point was well received by the Assembly. Again the issue of the complexity of being female and being superintendents came into view. The women were definitely aware that they had to be overtly strong and directive at times. The complexity centered around when and how these skills should be used. And while the women could point to times when choosing to use these skills was counterproductive and even dangerous, they understood that directing skills were an important part of their practice. Indeed, they believed that if they hadn't exhibited some of their directing skill, they would not have been hired in the first place.

It is not a surprise that school boards look for superintendents whom they believe to be "in charge" types. The "in charge" profile as a preferred construction of leadership permeates the literature—even the literature on collaborative decision making. The women of the Assembly were aware of the delicate balance between looking strong or "in charge" and working in collaboration to make decisions. They were in agreement, however, that acting in ways that were authoritarian or directive had to be saved for times when it was impossible to get groups together for collective decisions.

The Assembly agreed that success came when they worked supportively behind the scenes and in collaboration with others. They believed that they were beginning to understand the deeper meaning behind the collaborative practice of shared power.

PART THREE

MOTION

INTANGIBLES IN ACTION

The concluding part of the book shares the action that results as a byproduct when people impeccably practice the Seven Principles of Power. Further, it reveals these results in the work lives of the women superintendents in the study. These results, according to Castaneda, are final evidence that a person is practicing the Seven Principles.

Chapter 12 introduces the results of "Impeccable Practice." Chapters 13, 14, and 15 individually discuss each of the three results of impeccable practice. The final chapter in the section concludes the book by exploring what the book's message has meant for me at a personal level.

IMPECCABLE PRACTICE

THREE RESULTS

What matters is that a warrior be impeccable. . . .

—Carlos Castaneda, *Tales of Power*

Carlos Castaneda (1981) concluded his discussion of the Principles of Power by telling readers that there are three results for people who "impeccably" live the principles. I came to understand from my study that the women superintendents lived Castaneda's conclusion—the three results he referred to were evident in the "impeccable"—or what I call diligent and dedicated—practice of the women in the study.

Through my research with the twelve women superintendents, I found that the key to the Riddle of the Heart is a deep commitment to caring for and about others. Once a warrior discovers this key within herself, the "warrior's path" becomes available. The warrior's path consists of the impeccable practice of the seven Priniciples of Power. And the proof that a warrior has been impeccably practicing the principles is the manifestation, in her life, of three specific results (see Figure 1).

Castaneda (1981) explains just how important impeccability is to a warrior. He says that it is impeccable practice that protects a warrior from being under siege. For superintendents, being under siege comes in many forms—such as the pressure from multiple publics. The protection of impeccable practice occurs because a warrior has nothing in her personal possessions/character that can be used as leverage and, therefore, she cannot be threatened. In fact, a warrior has nothing in the world but her impeccablity and impeccablity cannot be threatened. Castaneda emphatically adds, however, that in a battle for one's life, a warrior should be prepared to strategically use every means possible to protect herself and should not ever count only on the protection of impeccable practice (215–216).

The three results of impeccable practice are that warriors: 1) "learn never to take themselves seriously; they learn to laugh at themselves, 2) learn to have endless patience, are never in a hurry; they never fret and, 3) learn to have an endless capacity to improvise" (Castaneda 1982, 291).

What Castaneda calls results are a warrior's states of mind achieved by the impeccable practice of the Principles of Power. The idea is that these states of mind are necessary components of success. Women superintendents in the study practiced these principles and arrived at these valued states of mind. The three results of their impeccable practice were constantly a part of their daily work.

What is interesting about the three results when compared to the Principles of Power, is that when the women talked about the results, they smiled. Their smiles were in contrast to their serious faces—the faces I saw when they talked about the parts of their practice that reflected the Principles of Power. I learned that while there was a great deal of struggle and effort in practicing the principles, the results of that impeccable practice produced happiness or even a type of ecstasy.

It was the experience of ecstasy that kept the women superintendents in their positions, kept them wanting more of the role, kept them, in a sense, "above the fray."

Rollo May (1975) discussed the source of ecstasy as being the union of *form and passion* with *order and vitality*. He made it clear that his use of the word was not in its popular sense of "hysteria," but in its

> historical, etymological sense of "ex-stasis"—that is, literally to "stand out from," to be freed from the usual split between subject and object which is a perpetual dichotomy in most human activity. *Ecstasy* is the accurate term for the intensity of consciousness that occurs in the creative act. But it is not to be thought of merely as a Bacchic "letting go"; it involves the total person, with the subconscious and unconscious acting in unity with conscious. It is not, thus, *irrational*; it is rather suprarational. It brings intellectual, volitional, and emotional functions into play all together. (49) [all original emphases]

And the ecstasy that I witnessed in the faces of the women superintendents, as they shared evidence that the three results were a part of their practice, was not of the hysterical variety. It was, instead, a result of the union of "form and passion" and "order and vitality," which were vividly explicit pieces of their practices as revealed in chapters 5 though 11.

When thinking about such a union—form and passion joined with order and vitality—it became clear to me that May (1975) posed a unique possibility. Elements of the suprarational—passion and vitality—are joined to rational structure—form and order—in this union. In my view, the suggestion that this type of union be a part of the practice of superintendents cannot be found in the literature. Instead, form and order stand alone.

Seeing form and order alone as the basis of leadership rests on the old notion that rational thinking can only occur when a person is passionless, even emotionless. Showing passion and emotion tends to be considered irrational behavior. Instead, behavior that is distant, cool, and in control is the normative standard for superintendents. In other words, behavior must have a definite form and must represent order or it is out of control, irrational.

For some reason, this idea continues to live on, at least covertly, even in the most recent books on superintendents of schools. For example, Sharp and Walter (1997) admonish superintendents, "You simply cannot allow personal attachments to mar your clear-headed ability to think and to reason" (147). In this directive, Sharp and Walter insist that superintendents remain emotionally uninvolved so that they can be rational. Surprisingly, research has shown for some time that this notion is erroneous. Consider that

> [t]here are data in Rorschach responses, for example, that indicate that people can more accurately observe precisely when they are emotionally involved—that is, reason works better when emotions are present; the person sees sharper and more accurately when his [her] emotions are engaged. Indeed, we cannot really see an object unless we have some emotional involvement with it. It may well be that reason works best in the state of ecstasy. (May 1975, 50)

In myriad ways, the women superintendents in the study are emotionally involved in their work. It is work of the heart. They are drawn to the work because they are emotionally involved in the lives of children and were willing to take tremendous risks and suffer emotional losses to be superintendents. They see things with a sharpness, a newness, and an honesty that hasn't been reflected in literature. And it is their emotional involvement in their work that propelled them through the struggles of the job and ultimately brought them deep enjoyment, a type of ecstasy.

The three results of impeccable practice—just like the principles—are deeply interconnected. One does not exist without the other. For example, the first result, humor or comedy, is an important part of creativity, the third result. As Kanter (1986) reminded us

> Every creative act is a form of play—playing with ideas, twisting the kaleidoscope of reality. Every new invention is a little bit irreverent: it challenges orthodoxy and treads on tradition. (12)

The ability to laugh at self—the first result—is humor at its best. It is the epitome of irreverence—allowing the warrior or superintendent to challenge orthodoxy and tread on tradition. In other words, to reshape or transform the role.

The ability to reshape or transform the role of the superintendency is heady stuff. And when reading about the impeccable practice of the women superintendents in the study, a reader might assume that the women themselves were arrogant or self-important. This was not the case. Because I interviewed people who worked with or knew the work of these women, I came to understand that the women were more humble than arrogant. Castaneda (1981) helped to explain this paradox when he wrote about the "unsurpassed humility" that a warrior feels when she is faced with the true poverty of her own human resources. And facing one's true poverty occurs when warriors realize that the odds against them are astonishing. The women in the study were pointedly aware that they were faced with astonishing odds, and as Castaneda described it, they had "no recourse but to step back and lower [their] heads" (222).

CHAPTER 13

FIRST RESULT

LAUGHING AT SELF

It was clear during visits with the successful women superintendents in the study that they laughed often. They were open, warm, and humorous. The literature on leadership is full of references to "a sense of humor" (see Bossert, Dwyer, Rowan, and Lee 1982; Brown and Irby 1998; Hill and Ragland 1995; Immegart 1988; Murphy 1988). But, as Lindle (1993) notes, few of these research studies focus specifically on what humor means for leaders and leadership.

While not grounded in research, discussions about the need for humor in specific areas of practice do appear in a few of the books about superintendents. For example, Konnert and Augenstein (1990) talk about humor as a part of the divergent thinking that is important for leaders and others in education. They state that educators and, in particular, administrators tend to be serious people and thus have a stifling effect on the playfulness that is necessary for divergent thinking.

Konnert and Augenstein (1990) suggest an exercise designed to help educators "see" how hard it is for them to "poke fun at professional problems, particularly those in which one has a personal stake" (84). The exercise is in two stages of brainstorming. In the first stage, small groups brainstorm solutions to a ridiculous problem like "how to keep bugs off a windshield." They note that a lot of laughter and far out ideas—with no critical remarks—will accompany this first stage of the exercise.

In the second stage of the exercise, the small groups brainstorm solutions to a real education problem. Konnert and Augenstein identify three things that usually happen in this second stage: "First, there [is] much

159

less humor during the brainstorming for this is serious business now. Second, there [is] some deviation from the brainstorming ground rule of no criticism of ideas. Third, not as many far-out ideas are generated" (84). The ability to poke fun at, or laugh at, self disappears, rendering the group much less creative and more self-important.

Lindle (1995) agrees with Konnert and Augenstein when she writes, "[w]ith laughter comes relaxation. With relaxation comes mental freedom. With mental freedom come the agility of mind so necessary for reflection on and invention of new definitions and solutions to changing problems of school leadership" (262). She goes farther, explaining the far-reaching effects of laughter when she asserts that

> students of educational administration can become accustomed to the topsy-turvy moments of practice. As future school leaders turn assumptions upside down and inside out [in ways that make them laugh] in an effort to redefine problems and search for innovative solutions, they will not only have opportunities to practice inventive and creative thinking; they will also practice the very necessary skills of thinking on their feet in the increasingly contested realm of educational decision making. (263)

It is the ability to laugh at yourself that Castaneda identifies as one of the results of practicing the Seven Principles. He writes that when warriors can laugh at themselves, it is a sign that they take themselves less seriously than most people—something required for warriors. Melendez (1996) agrees with Castaneda in the statement that "a sense of humor and the ability to throw back their heads and laugh at themselves are essential for leaders" (302). She laments the fact that corporations find it necessary to hire consultants to help their staff play and use humor.

When people can laugh at themselves, they do not view themselves as superior. Instead they are humble and thus more able to take in all of the information needed to survive in the most difficult of circumstances. Ego is no longer an issue: it does not need protection.

The women in the study noted that they had learned not to take themselves seriously. Often, their humor centered on the incongruity of being female in a traditionally male role. In other words, they had learned to laugh at themselves. One woman said,

> Well, once in a while I think the fact that you're a woman just sort of "pops" up. It could be from a comment that somebody else made, for instance, we have our little favorite joke we use around here. And it came out of a situation earlier this summer,

and it referred to a couple of "skirts" running the district. Maybe a tough decision gets made and I will quip, "Well, you've got to remember a 'skirt' made that decision"—or something like that [laughter]. So I think having a good sense of humor and being able to laugh at yourself a little bit in the situation—I am a woman and wear a skirt. . . .

Another woman had a similar story:

> I don't have a big thing about this "women" thing. I know some women superintendents who I really don't like to spend time with because they're always into this thing about, well, because I am a woman, this is the way they treated me. To me that's ridiculous. You're a person, [laugh] and you build those relationships so you don't have that kind of stuff. . . . [A]nd we kid about that. I mean, at the end of a meeting I will say, everybody, let's clean up. And I'll pick up the cups and do stuff. People who don't know me that well sometimes will say, "The superintendent does this cleaning?" I say, "What difference does it make, you know, we're all in this together."

As can be seen in the quotes above, the women in the study used humor to maintain their mental, emotional, and physical balance and health while in the position. This is not a new idea. Medical care workers of all types have for some time known the value of laughter for health and healing.

Meyer (1997) states that research has shown that laughter and a positive attitude can be healing. It bolsters the immune system and may lead people to take better care of themselves. Anger, negative thinking, and stress do the reverse (72).

Alice Dormar, author of *Healing mind, healthy woman* (1997), believes that negative thinking results from programming during childhood. It was clear to me that most of the women in the study had experienced positive "can do" messages from significant people during their childhood (see chapter 8). These "can do" attitudes were kept alive and firmly intact with the women's senses of humor even when they experienced the "to be expected" attacks from the public and from others in various positions in education.

Add the stresses of gender to the somewhat common elements of anger and stress experienced by superintendents and the importance of the role of humor escalates. The women understood the role of humor and some reported that they had learned to laugh at themselves through a conscious effort. It took time. One superintendent said:

> I think I have truly learned to laugh at myself. It had something to do with my learning that I am centered and focused. When I understood those things about myself I was more comfortable and less vulnerable. I could find the humor in what I saw so I could go ahead and stay true to my focus and accomplish the task that lay before me. For me, it has been a learned skill. It has come with a certain maturity of experience.

This woman's comment reminded me that "laughing at self" for warriors comes as a result of practicing the Seven Principles. It is a culmination of experience over time and represents, as she said, a "certain maturity."

THE ASSEMBLY

There was a difference in the way the Assembly talked about the three results of impeccable practice as compared to their discussions of the Seven Principles. This difference lies in the fact that, as a researcher, I was not observing or hearing about their individual lives and professional practices so there was no way for me to observe the *results* of their impeccable practice. The only way the Assembly could talk about the results was in the same way they discussed the principles. They talked as if the three results were the means to an end rather than the end. Their conversations, however, are useful because they helped me view the results from many different perspectives.

One of the superintendents in the Assembly remarked that laughing made her more human in the eyes of others. She continued, "Because we're in a male role, we're often seen as not human—not like everyone else. And so, if we can laugh, then we're more human." Others agreed. Another woman went farther,

> I think that learning to laugh at ourselves also fits into the brain research that tells us that laughter releases a chemical in the brain that does several things. One, it helps us learn more. It also helps us relax. It helps us be more aware of the world around us. So, there is a biological and a biochemical reason for needing laughter in our lives.

The discussion continued. One superintendent said, " Laughter is encouraged by doctors especially for anyone with a serious illness. I think we do a lot of laughing for our own healing—something we need constantly because of the stress we are under."

Another superintendent reported that she had heard about the necessity of laughter in a recent conference. She shared,

I just got back from the new superintendents' conference and at one of the sessions, the president of the organization gave us a talk. He said, "I'm going to give you tips for being superintendents." His number one tip was to be able to laugh at yourself. I mean to not take yourself so seriously. He said that the one thing he wished he could have known earlier was about laughing at himself. He said he made some mistakes, and could look back at the times when he took everything so seriously and got himself in trouble or in uncomfortable situations.

I think that maybe learning to laugh at ourselves as women might be easier than it is for men because we haven't been taught to protect our egos as much. We would rather diffuse a situation rather than to escalate it. And humor can be used for that.

Others began to think of ways that humor was useful. One superintendent said,

I think to be able to laugh at yourself puts others at ease especially in situations where you are asking them to try new things or put themselves on the line. Laughter makes us more human and helps encourage others to participate and understand that life is just not that serious. The sun will come up the next morning. So learning to laugh at yourself becomes one of your greatest assets.

Another superintendent reflected on the nature of her position and how it almost required her to take herself lightly when she said,

I think that any of us who get into these jobs are by nature hard workers. And so, we commit a lot of ourselves to our jobs. And when you do that, when you put in sixty or more hours, you are doing that so you won't make mistakes and to avoid criticism. In fact, you tend to believe that putting in the time will stop criticism. [Everyone laughed at this point.] So when things don't go exactly how you had planned or as you expected, laughing at yourself is really important. You can say to yourself, "I did everything possible, and the outcome was not what I anticipated, but, oh well, I'll try it again or I'll be back at it." You kind of laugh at your own expectations and it becomes uplifting in your own thought process. It changes your mental perspective.

I do think it is a very difficult thing to do because we are so heavily invested in things going a certain way after all of our work. So, I think the ability to laugh is a great gift. And I think it is probably easier for some than others. If you look at our male colleagues and some of the people that would be your mentors, some of them have pretty uplifting attitudes about things. They are always quipping about something or taking things a little bit lighter. The ones that are real serious all of the time about everything, you would probably not seek out. So, if we recognize that in other people, we have to realize that's probably how people are thinking about us, too. I think it's a skill. And I think if you don't have it automatically, it is something to work very hard at. It makes your life easier and makes life easier for those around you, too.

The talk moved to the topic of how the women had learned to laugh at themselves. One woman offered her story:

I know exactly how I learned to laugh at myself. I have a marvelous staff who helped me. I have that Scandinavian heritage which makes me stoic by nature, and I tend to take myself seriously. So, this one was really hard to learn. But I have the good fortune of having people around me who have marvelous senses of humor. They helped me move beyond my seriousness.

The day I knew I had begun to catch on, I was on the phone and suddenly looked up to see a half dozen faces at my doorway. I stopped and said, "Okay, what's up?" And they said, "Well, look at your shoes." I'd gotten up at five that morning, didn't want to disturb my husband, and reached in my closet and got the shoes. And they matched, they were both the same style, but one was rose and one was black. And, I was forty-eight miles from home. [Everyone laughed.] I read somewhere that Dan Rather did the same thing once. I laughed at myself, genuinely, that day, and I noticed it.

But the staff helped me enormously. I give that staff a lot of credit for putting up with me for so many years before I learned. Maybe they saw that I needed to learn to lighten up. I really remember that as the day I was first able to laugh at myself. I think they made me feel secure as an administrator, and that it was okay to laugh at yourself. That you don't lose anything when you do it, you gain enormously.

Another superintendent added:

I think we really need people in our lives who help us move beyond the stuff we are dealing with that we take so seriously. Even when we go home at night, we're still there and the problems go through our heads at two in the morning, and we know we can pull people together in the morning to solve the problems, but we still won't let go. We need someone either in our work life or our personal life to hold up the mirror, and who knows us well enough to say, "I think you're really worried about this. You know, let it go, it's time to laugh."

One of the women smiled and said,

> Now I know why I have my husband of thirty-one years. He is the person for me who knows how to make light of things. Sometimes I'll get mad at him and accuse him of trying to make a joke of everything. And he does. He has a gift for that. And it keeps things balanced. . . . I find myself laughing sometimes in the strangest situations. People, I'm sure, think I'm losing it. But I see things sometimes that are just so bizarre, I just have to laugh. I just don't know what else to do about it, so I laugh.

A central office administrator, who did a lot of hiring, talked about how her ideas about humor affected her work.

> Two of the most important things I look for when I hire teachers are, one, I look for a person with a sense of humor. I think they can do a lot more for the kids. The kids relate to them better. The second one is flexibility. And, we ought to have these same attributes if we value them enough to make hiring decisions based on them.

A superintendent ended the discussion by identifying the things in her makeup that for a while prevented her from begin able to laugh at herself. Her words were instructive for all of us. She said,

> I think that being able to laugh at yourself requires—at least in my case—some personal growth and giving up some perfectionist tendencies—and defensiveness. I think the two are very closely associated—whether you are having to prove yourself in a position or personally. I don't think that I had the ability to laugh at myself until I released some of those characteristics and found a different focus that gave me permission to make mistakes and then to learn from those mistakes for the future.

Again, as I heard this woman speak, I was reminded of the way the Seven Principles created this result. This superintendent was almost laying out a road map of her work through several of the principles. For one, she had learned to "fear nothing"—to let go of her fear of being less than perfect—to give up the need to protect her ego—in order to laugh at herself. When ego takes a back seat, people can laugh at themselves, be patient as the second result reflects, and innovative as the third result claims. It struck me just how interconnected the impeccable practice of the Principles of Power is to their results.

CHAPTER 14

SECOND RESULT

PATIENCE WITHOUT FRETTING

Of all the chapters in this book, chapter 11 most vividly relates examples of the women superintendents' patience. Without a doubt, patience is tested by collaborative decision making. And the women superintendents in the study found that making decisions any other way—although sometimes necessary—was most often counterproductive. Making decisions quickly and alone in areas of importance created larger problems—which stole time later. Knowing this actuality made them patient enough to take the time for consensus building. As one woman told me:

> I spend a lot of time—some critical time—trying to get a sense of who the key players are, the stakeholders, and how things happen in the community.

Another shared:

> My guess is that people would view me as being stronger at consensus building [as a decision-making style]. . . . I am a process person—probably to a fault.

When I asked one woman whether she found women had more patience to take the necessary time to look at more sides of a problem and were, therefore, more responsive than men, she replied:

> One hundred percent more! . . . . I think women look at not only the objective things but also the affective things of what's going on in schools. When they're dealing with kids I think men are much more capable of separating, and I call it compartmentalizing what goes on in their lives, their family is one

and the work is one, you know. I think for women, it all kind
of melds together. (Of course, there are men who look at the
"affective things of . . . school.")

Another woman talked about how hard it was to finally experience
the patience as a result of her impeccable practice of the Seven Principles.
She mused:

> I am a compulsive first-born type, so patience didn't come
> easily. I had to learn it. It is sort of a mark of maturity that
> came over time because of lots of different experiences where I
> had to endure and survive. For me, learning about patience
> came with a shift in my beliefs to a place where I understood
> that there are multiple desirable outcomes to most issues. And
> once I understood that, my thinking began to focus on strength-
> ening processes that would support that idea. So, for me now,
> it is my responsibility to support and identify processes where
> multiple outcomes can be explored and experienced. For me, I
> had to acquire centeredness and focus to gain true patience. It
> can't be just on the outside, it has to be all through me.

The words "acquire centeredness" caught my attention as I listened
to this woman. According to Tom Crum (1994), centeredness is a "true
psychophysiological phenomenon that affects everything in your environment. It may appear difficult to comprehend on an intellectual level.
It is only through experiencing centering that it can be comprehensible
and useful" (97).

Crum relates that centering is a form of mind/body integration, an
experience in which the mind and body are intimately connected, and it
can be achieved through simple exercises. It is through the practice of
centeredness—full commitment and concentration—that great athletes,
artists, and professionals perform at optimum levels. Further, it is the
uncomfortable moments when conflict arises that provide the best opportunities to test the power of a centered state. When centered, Crum says,
"you'll find that it is impossible to be angry, fearful, or at the mercy of
the conflict in any emotional or physical way" (98). When considering
this information, it is easy to understand why the woman quoted above
connected centeredness with the patience she had learned.

All of the women in the study reported and exhibited a full commitment to and concentration on their work. Perhaps they were experiencing centeredness even without knowing it. Crum (1994) suggests that
this is a possibility. People who operate at optimum level, who are fully
committed and concentrated on the job, are operating from centeredness

and yet not thinking about it. Such a state, he says, optimizes our own progress toward excellence (98). And, patience without fretting is certainly evidence of progress toward excellence.

THE ASSEMBLY

While the idea of patience without fretting sounded wonderful to the women of the Assembly, they felt it was a hard won state of being. And as I noted in chapter 13, because the goal of the Assembly was to discuss the principles and the three results, rather than an effort to examine individual practices, the readers will find some narrative that reflects the struggles with gaining these results. These struggles are real for everyone who is practicing the Seven Principles. The results do not come quickly or easily. But they do come as a manifestation of practicing the Seven Principles.

One superintendent realistically stated the obvious when she said,

> For me, this is a very, very difficult concept to internalize because when working in schools you are always attending to a schedule. We start school on a certain day, before you know it we have parent conferences, then it's Christmas, and finally right into graduation. And then you start all over again. And so, you are always push, push, pushing to make certain you meet one deadline or another. For sure, every month, there's at least one board meeting—you have to get out the agenda on time and it has to be posted on a certain day. So the whole job is calendar driven. Because of that, it is really hard to have patience with people when you have deadlines and they don't meet your deadlines, and things get postponed—for me it is very difficult. Certainly I know that it is important and I can see how great leaders have this characteristic, but for me it's very difficult and still very important.

Another superintendent approached the topic in a unique way. She understood the term *fretting* in a different way than others in the group. She stated:

> I think that one of the ways I get to the answers in my mind is through fretting. I struggle, think through, or fret over issues. And then usually at two A.M. I find the answer to something I've struggled with. So, if I eliminated fretting, I would have to resign. But I do think that this message is an important one for the external self, because if you convey anxiety to everyone who's working around you, you are poisoning aspects of the work environment. And I think that this message of patience

without fretting is a good reminder for me that while I may use fretting internally, I need to have enormous patience with people as we work through problems in the system. Anxiety is not a very inviting environment to work in.

Another superintendent joined her:

I agree with what you're saying. It's almost like you have two selves. The external one through which you give the appearance that this will be okay, that this will pass. The phrase I use is "make like a duck." You know the old saying, "look calm on top, but paddling like hell underneath." That's my philosophy. And so I do that with the staff on the surface. But in those private moments, then I do what I call "worry with it," or I *fret*. I don't use the word fret, but I worry with something the way you would with worry beads. You know, I feel it all over, I turn it around. I look at the situation from every angle and then the answer just comes to me. It's a strength, I think, having the ability to have it just come to me that way.

I joined the conversation at that point because I was really interested in the phenomenon they were referring to as well as the language they were using. I thought that we needed to explore the meaning of the word *fret* so that we all understood each other. I offered my understanding and said,

For me, the word *fret* means useless thought, and what I hear you talking about is certainly not that. You are talking about an actual process that I think is very, very useful. Would you agree that there may be a separation of useless worry and what you are doing that is so helpful? It feels like you are dumping information into your minds and letting it stew— and you may not even be aware of the thought process, but an answer comes to the top. You can feel it happening even though you can't describe it with words. From what I understand about creativity, that is a creative process. It is a very engaging thing. You are almost consumed with it, but it has a positive outcome.

On the other hand, I think that Castaneda used the term fret to mean worrying uselessly or obsessing over something that nothing can be done about. One person I know called it "sawing sawdust." He said, "Don't saw sawdust, saw wood."

Another superintendent offered,

I think that there is a continuum of thought that moves between creative thought that is engaging in productive activity and the opposite type of thought that is obsessive fretting. And we probably move along that continuum every hour of every day in some ways.

Tying patience with fretting was the next connection made in the conversation. One woman suggested that

> in terms of the continuum of thought, we talked about productive stewing versus the fretting. I think that emotion plays a part in the difference in the two. I think that fretting almost has an air of despair while stewing has a sense of empowerment that you have when you know you can pull the resources together to help get through to find multiple solutions. And that is where the patience comes in. If in that moment you have the patience to wait for the multiple solutions, then you don't get into the despair. Despair won't take over because if you have patience you know that over time you will get the power that comes with finding solutions.

One woman made an observation about the times when she found herself wasting energy on fretting. She said,

> I find myself fretting when I take on too much at one time. At those times, I find myself sort of walking in circles and accomplishing nothing. Not only in my actions, but also in my thoughts. I'm not able to focus. Then as I begin to think through that and sort it through, then I get more to the other end of the continuum where I'm putting aside those things that I can't do anything about—like is suggested by one of the principles. I eliminate them so they won't complicate my thought waves—so to speak.

One of the superintendents changed the direction of our conversation by shifting to a different perspective on patience. She began,

> We've been focusing on the fretting part, and there's a patience part to the second result that I think is really important, too. Our world is ambiguous so we are not able to directly control things. Because of that, having patience is an art form that we need to exercise—something that we need to learn more how to do. We need to focus in a way that blots out the turmoil when someone comes into our offices and we have fifteen projects going on. We have to be able to put the phone down, put all the papers down, and sit and look at them eye to eye and focus on their issue. That requires discipline and patience. We tend to want to bring resolution to things in a world that really has no resolution. Knowing that definitely requires patience or we drive ourselves crazy.

The women then turned their attention to stories of how they learned that patience was an important part of their work. One woman started,

I can remember working for a superintendent who hammered on me for about eight years about being patient. If there's one thing I remember about him, it's the fact that he kept saying, "Be patient, be patient." And, he had the gift of patience. He had two rules that he lived by. Number one, don't make decisions when you are angry, and number two, don't make decisions on a Friday afternoon. On Friday afternoons, he told everyone that he would be in his office fishing. He invited people to come to his office to sit back, put up their feet, reflect, and brainstorm. It was an incredible luxury and yet, he got a tremendous amount of things done.

And I think about that and realize that it is extremely important to have the patience to let the stew just stew instead of fret. You have to let it just stew. You can't look for a quick fix or react to turmoil when you're doing that because you are calm. You are letting the stew simmer and boil a little bit. You are right, we have to remain calm. Because the minute the bus pulls up with thirty-five kids on it and they just got rear-ended and now the kids are talking about headaches, the staff will look to you to remain calm. The minute I get a little bit anxious, my secretary starts getting a little anxious and the tenseness starts increasing and you say "Whoa!" So patience is something you absolutely have to have.

Another woman told her story. It involved her learning about patience and decision making. As she told it,

> The first job I ever had was as an assistant principal to a principal who was my first mentor. At first my relationship with him was difficult because I was so impatient. I had all these wonderful ideas and things I wanted to do. He seemed to me to be the most wishy-washy person, someone who was unable to make a decision. I was used to the type of administrator who told you like it was. This man was just the opposite. He would always sit back and reflect and think about it. I mean it could be days. He would talk to all kinds of people and then he'd come back and talk to me and I would feel like, "Oh, I can't take it, I would have done that immediately. We have wasted so much time."
>
> Of course, what happened was that there were many times when he saved my butt because I made some really stupid decisions before I heard other opinions. My impatience made me a poor listener. I wasn't really listening or even interested in listening to everything at the time because I thought I knew everything [all laughing]. Finally I learned patience, and I learned it from him during the three years I worked with him.

Another superintendent agreed that impatience can create difficulty. She said,

> I think all of us have been in situations where we haven't been patient and we've said things that we regret. At times when stress is high and we lose our cool, we say things and we realize that we really blew it. So after a few of those moments you learn the wisdom of being patient with people. You learn that.
>
> I think the part of not fretting is also learned. The way I understand fretting is that it is that destructive kind of thinking. I know when I've entered into the fret mode. [All laugh.] And usually when that happens the stress level has pretty well topped out, and there have been lots of different challenges that have occurred, and I lay in bed and I can't think. All I can do is just kind of zero in on this one little thing over and over and over. I know it's not helping. I know I want to sleep. I know I want to have a life. I know I want to be happy. So then I try to draw the line. I need to stop this. It is not helping. So that is when I say, "Okay, I need to exercise," and that helps. Anything to get out of that fret mode.

As the women of the Assembly talked about the importance of patience, they made it clear that impeccably practicing the Seven Principles was critical. Patience as an end result of practicing the principles was well worth choosing to take the warrior's path.

CHAPTER 15

THIRD RESULT

IMPROVISATION

The women superintendents in the study were extremely aware of their own ability to improvise. In fact, they knew that as women, improvisation was a requirement of the position. Some of them told stories that uncovered the strong need for improvisation due to gender. One woman very good-naturedly offered this story as an example of how she learned that it was important to have the ability to improvise:

It was hard for a lot of people to deal with me [as a woman]. There's no question about that [laughing]. I just wasn't an "old boy," you know. . . . So people were watchful of me . . . . There was a lot of monitoring and questions like, "You wouldn't think of doing that would you?" and "You haven't thought of this, have you?" And, "You wouldn't give them that, would you?"

Q. And you think this happened more than it does to men?

A. Yes, because I had observed the previous [male] superintendent for ten years. . . . I don't think people felt they had to tell him to watch out for this or watch out for that.

The literature on the superintendency and on leaders, in general, discusses the need for creativity. In some literature, creativity is explored under the topic of "divergent thinking" (Konnert and Augenstein 1990). "Novel or innovative ideas do not spring from a vacuum; rather, they come from the novel combination of knowledge and/or experiences stored in one's mind," state Konnert and Augenstein (82). Certainly the superintendents in the study could hold several perspectives simultaneously in their minds—which resulted in their creative thinking.

Not only were the women aware of the necessity to be able to improvise, they seemed to enjoy this aspect of their jobs. One woman stated:

> I think that the fact that we need to improvise is why I like the job. Every day is different, and when there's a challenge, I actually get to use my ability to be creative.

Improvisation and creativity are directly connected. The first definition of "improvise" is "to invent . . . ." (*The American Heritage Dictionary* 1981, 662). And the mother of invention is creativity. Several of the principles contribute to the ability to improvise and be creative. Principle Six, Risk Taking, is an inherent part of creativity. Courage is required to take the risks necessary to be creative or to invent. Rollo May (1975) discussed the type of courage that is needed to be creative when he wrote, "Courage is . . . the capacity to move ahead in spite of despair" (3).

The women in the study had this type of courage (see chapter 10). They had what May (1975) refers to as "creative courage" (14). Creative courage, he wrote, "is the discovering of new forms, new symbols, new patterns on which a new society can be built" (15). He continued,

> Every profession can and does require some creative courage. In our day, technology and engineering, diplomacy, business, and certainly teaching, all of these professions and scores of others are in the midst of radical change and require courageous persons to appreciate and direct this change. The need for creative courage is in direct proportion to the degree of change the profession is undergoing. (15)

To be sure, the superintendency is changing. In fact, having women in the position is in and of itself a change. It is no wonder, then, that the women in the study were well acquainted with creative practices or improvisation. They are, themselves, new forms of the superintendency. Their practice is a new symbol, a new pattern on "which a new society [and new profession] can be built" (May 1975, 15).

Many of the new patterns in the practice of the women superintendents have been reflected in other chapters in this book. The stories about how they improvised were varied and numerous.

The women in the study constantly relied on their ability to improvise in order to make do with the materials at hand and still do things in a creative way. One reflected on how she was viewed by a colleague:

> She calls me "Lemonade Mary" [not actual first name]—you
> know, someone who makes lemonade out of lemons.

The ability that women educational leaders have to make "lemonade out
of lemons" is referred to in Hill and Ragland's (1995) book, *Women as
Educational Leaders*. They state:

> Regardless of how the positions finally come their way, women
> have often metaphorically taken lemons and produced lemon-
> ade. They have gained valuable experience and impressed
> others with the competence of women effectively handling
> crises or critical administrative roles. . . . Achieving the seem-
> ingly impossible gave women the chance to learn new skills,
> extend their visibility, gain job advancement, and make posi-
> tive contributions. One woman recalled receiving a promotion
> in another system because the job she had previously accom-
> plished demonstrated her ability to successfully "do things
> differently." (22)

Doing things differently is the hallmark of creativity and improvisation. Their new patterns of practice made the women superintendents
in the study not only unusual, but also successful. They enjoyed the third
result of the impeccable practice of the Seven Principles of Power. They
enjoyed improvising, creating, and inventing.

THE ASSEMBLY

Most of the women in the Assembly had experienced the manifestation
of this result in their work lives, so the discussion that focused on improvisation was an upbeat one. The fact that their work required creativity
and invention was something that made them smile. As one superintendent said:

> I think that's why we stay with the job. At least that's why I
> stay with the job. Because every day isn't the same and when
> there's a challenge we actually get to use the creative side of
> the brain. And those automatic pilot, mundane things that we
> have to do at the board meetings—all those things that you
> have to do every month, and you make sure you do all of that.
> That's on one side of my brain and on one side of my desk.
> Then on the other side are the things that actually take some
> creative thought. And I've even looked forward to those days.
> I sometimes welcome crisis or controversy because I can solve
> them through creativity. And that's why we stay in the posi-
> tion, because we can do those things.

This woman's comments echoed Bennis (1989) when he stated that in his conversations with exceptional leaders in all fields, the need for "right-brain qualities came up again and again" (105). As an example, he quoted Gloria Steinem who said, "It helps if you're a nonlinear thinker. . . . [W]e put together things that haven't gone together in the past. . . . To me, the model of progress is not linear" (105). The idea of nonlinear thinking was expressed in myriad ways by the women of the Assembly.

One of the superintendents talked about the extreme need for women, in particular, to be creative and improvise. As she put it,

> I think the increased challenge that we have as women in this role is that not only do we have to draw upon our creativity and our ability to improvise in our work, but we also continue to try to juggle a lot of the demands of family life and integrate that somehow into our work lives. And I think that doing that takes another level of creativity. You want to be at your child's game or you want to make or buy something or prepare food in some way that fits. And if you still carry all the expectations of what you may have done for all of your life before the superintendency, there's a lot of improvisation that has to take place to juggle all of that.

One of the assistant superintendents thought that improvisation was necessary because surprises filled every day. She believed that improvisation, in part, was evident in her ability to be flexible. She asserted:

> I don't think you could do your job if you weren't flexible. There's just no way in the world that you can predict your day. And I fill in for the superintendent when she is gone, and I have learned that everything that she has to remember is just an incredible task. Flexibility has to be the number one thing that the job requires.

Another woman agreed with her:

> I have to agree with you. That's why I love the job. I love going to work in the morning and not knowing what the day holds. And knowing that you're going to have to improvise. In order to survive, you have to improvise. And, I would venture to say that everyone here is highly skilled at not only juggling and being flexible, but improvising as you go through the day.
>
> Whether it's to problem solve or it's to deal with something major that just came up unexpectedly. Or you get the call from the state, and they want a form or a document that you don't have, so you improvise. But I also think it's probably

the one thing that creates my desire to be a superintendent. The superintendency gives me the opportunity and the reason to find that skill in myself. And when I look back on my career path, it is easy to see that routine kinds of things are not for me. I enjoy the unexpected and the fact that I know I can deal with it. Don't you think, in fact, that we would all still be in our first classroom positions if we didn't love to improvise and be creative in the face of the unexpected?

There was strong agreement among the Assembly members. They all appeared to like or even love this aspect of the superintendency. One superintendent explained why:

It gives me an adrenaline rush. I don't know if others here experience that. I think that happens because what I am doing hasn't been done before or I haven't figured out how to get it accomplished before.

Another woman shared her insight:

This desire to be creative is probably the reason I hate forms so much. You know, we get those forms from the state or whatever, and they don't give you any room to be creative. I hate forms. They give you just one way to do that stuff, and I think that's the reason we get so angry with the state department. They want us to do things in only one way when our jobs are never the same from day to day.

A third superintendent explained why the opportunities to improvise were so important to her:

I think we long for those moments and cherish them because when we do solve a problem, when we have improvised, for that moment, we have the recognition, and we have a feeling of accomplishment that almost feels real. You can't make it into a plaque, but it's almost tangible. And I think that is what validates us.

The women of the Assembly made it clear that improvising was a delightful necessity. They loved being in a position that required creativity.

So now, when people ask me why anyone would want to be a superintendent, I quickly answer, "They are people who need to express themselves in creative ways, and the superintendency is a position that insists on that type of expression."

CHAPTER 16

CASTANEDA AND ME

In my opinion, Estes (1992) expressed beautifully how intangible concepts become internalized and then become explicit in our work, when she wrote, "Our work is to show we have been breathed upon—to show it, give it out, sing it out, to live out in the topside world what we have received through our sudden knowings from story, from body, from dreams and journeys of all sorts" (33).

Although I have never been a superintendent of schools, at one time I aspired to the position; therefore, my connection to the women superintendents through research has personal implications. And I have changed as a result. The ways I view the world and am in the world have changed. I was shaken during my conversations with the women superintendents who shared the stories of their dreams and journeys. I became alerted to the skill and finesse of these women in positions of power, as well as to my feelings of pride that I am a woman.

As I have come to understand, it is the intensely emotional stories which transfix and change us—which "present the knife of insight, the flame of the passionate life, the breath to speak what one knows, [and] the courage to stand what one sees without looking away . . . " (Estes 1992, 21).

I write to speak what I know—what I have come to know as my "truth"—and it is with the help of Castaneda (1981) that I found the "courage to stand what [I] see without looking away." As a student of Castaneda's, I have applied the Seven Principles of Power to my practice as a postadministrator, professor/researcher/writer. The three results of my using the Seven Principles follow like those reflected in the book.

First, I *laugh* at myself as a "postmodern wanna-be." While struggling to work within my idea of postmodernism, I constantly bump into rigid constructions of self. A language full of dualisms and omnipotent utterings betrays me in a shameless fashion. I must finally admit that I was born and bred a positivist, with little hope of experiencing the divorce I seek. Thus, I laugh at my efforts as they tend to turn on me again and again. It is in my laughter that freedom comes.

Second, I am willing to wait for my "voice" to fully develop—something that, I am now convinced cannot be hurried. My voice has been silent for most of life, and as with all growth processes, there is no way to hurry its maturity. While working as a teacher and a principal, my patience was deepened because of my work with developing students. While working as a professor of educational administration, the deepening continues. It is time to turn patience inward toward myself so that I can develop fully.

Finally, it is through the use of metaphor that I, as a woman writer/ researcher, *improvise* to share research in a softer style—one that is more intuitively inclusive, I hope. In doing so, joining the spirit of the women in the study with research becomes possible. Research enlivened with spirit can only be captured in metaphor and only metaphor can illuminate the complexities of reality that are beyond logic. Further, I embrace the promise that metaphors hold for eliminating some of the complexity accompanying the articulation—oral and written—of gender-related research.

Through the process of writing a book that uses metaphor, I have come to understand that the key to the Riddle of the Heart is caring for and about others. By using this key, I find myself on the path of the warrior, struggling to impeccably practice the Seven Principles of Power. I rest assured that through my practice, three results that I value will manifest themselves in my life. Life becomes a joyous challenge. And as Fields (1994) notes,

> In order to meet this challenge, warriors throughout the world always have cultivated certain qualities and values: courage and bravery in facing both life and death; discipline in training both body and mind; strategy in keeping and restoring peace, as well as in battle; knowledge of one's own weakness and strength, as well as of the opponent's; and loyalty to comrades, as well as to a transcendent value. (xv)

ABOUT THE AUTHOR

C. Cryss Brunner is an assistant professor in the department of educational administration at the University of Wisconsin-Madison. She completed her Ph.D. at the University of Kansas in 1993. Her research on women, power, the superintendency, and the gap between public schools and their communities has appeared in such journals as *Educational Policy, Journal for a Just and Caring Education, The Journal of Educational Administration, Policy Studies Journal, The School Administrator, Educational Considerations, Contemporary Education,* and *The Journal of School Leadership.* Her edited book *Sacred dreams: Women and the superintendency* was published by State University of New York Press in 1999.

Brunner is the 1996–97 recipient of the National Academy of Education's Spencer Fellowship for her work on the relationship between superintendents' definitions of power and decision-making processes. She is the 1998 recipient of the University Council for Educational Administration's Jack Culbertson Award for her outstanding contributions to the field as a junior professor. In addition, she serves as joint director of the UCEA Joint Program Center for the Study of the Superintendency.

NOTES

CHAPTER 1

1. See for example: Capra, F., *The Tao of physics: An exploration of the parallels between modern physics and Eastern mysticism.* Berkeley: Shambhala, 1975, 161.

CHAPTER 2

1. One of the limitations of this study is the absence of women of color. Too often gender generalities are based on the experiences of white middle-class women (Spelman 1988). As my sample grows over time, I have been able to add women of color.

2. Three steps of organizing the data into taxonomies included unitizing, categorizing, and relating. The purpose of *unitizing* was to identify and record essential information units. A unit is a single piece of information able to stand by itself: it is self-explanatory (Hosti 1969, in Herzog 1986; Skrtic 1985). Every interview was divided into units of information with each unit coded with a designation for the respondent. Coding was done in order that the item's content could be traced back to raw field or interview notes while preserving the confidentiality of the participants.

Categorizing was done to bring those units relating to the same content together into a loose taxonomy. Units were physically separated into separate files on the computer and sorted into groups or categories of similar content.

Relating was done after the units were categorized. Each category was analyzed in terms of its relationship to other categories. I used a system of color coding the material and posted memos to myself (Glaser & Strauss 1967; Strauss 1987) in order to reflect constantly on what relationships or connections I was developing. After analysis, related categories were placed into taxonomies.

CHAPTER 3

1. It is important to note that most of Castaneda's books refer to as many women apprenticed warriors as men.

CHAPTER 4

1. Although the term *stalking* currently carries negative connotations, it is not meant to be negative within the context of Castaneda's work or within the context of this book.

2. Some feminists have been critical of the views of women and caring held by Gilligan (1982) and Noddings (1984). These feminists are critical of any essentialized notion of women (Weiler 1988, cited in Ladson-Billings 1995, 473) and suggest that no empirical evidence exists to support the notion that women care in ways different from men or that any such caring informs their scholarship and work.

CHAPTER 5

1. Susan Chase is one of the few. See Chase, S., *Ambiguous empowerment: The work narratives of women school superintendents*. Amherst: University of Massachusetts Press, 1995.

CHAPTER 10

1. Research by H. M. Marks, and K. Seashore-Louis, in *Educational Evaluation and Policy Analysis* 19 (3): 245–275, has shown that while collaborative cultures are necessary for improved academic performance, collaboration itself must be focused on academic achievement and instruction in order for improved academic achievement to occur.

CHAPTER 11

1. While stressing the contributions of female power theorists, I recognize that some men have also recognized the importance of "power with/to." For example, Talcott Parsons (1969) has argued that power should be regarded as the capacity of a social system to achieve its collective goals, Clarence Stone (1989) has argued that power involves the capacity for social production as well as for social control, and Thomas Wartenberg (1990) has analyzed "transformative power." Because I wish to avoid oversimplifications such as positing the existence of a male conception of power and a female conception of power, I sometimes use the terminology of men who have contributed to the concept of "power with/to."

REFERENCES

Adler, S., J. Laney, and M. Packer. 1993. *Managing women: Feminism and power in educational management.*

The American Heritage Dictionary of the English Language. 1981. Boston: Houghton Mifflin Company.

Andrews, L. 1993. *Woman at the edge of two worlds: The spiritual journey through menopause.* New York: HarperCollins Publishers.

Arendt, H. 1972. On violence. In *Crises of the Republic.* New York: Harcourt, Brace, Jovanovitch.

Arnez, N. L. 1981. *The besieged school superintendent: A case study of school superintendent and school board relations in Washington, D. C., 1973–75.* Washington, D.C.: University Press of America.

Arrien, A. 1993. *The four-fold way: Walking the paths of the warrior, teacher, healer, and visionary.* San Francisco: HarperCollins Publishers.

Arrien, A. 1994. Accessing power. In Fields, R. (Ed.). *The awakened warrior: Living with courage, compassion, and discipline,* 109–111. New York: G. P. Putnam's Sons.

Astin, H. S., and C. Leland. 1991. *Women of influence, women of vision: A cross-generational study of leaders and social vision.* San Francisco: Jossey-Bass Publishers.

Bachrach, P., and M. S. Baratz. 1962. Two faces of power. *American Political Science Review* 57: 947–952.

Baker, P. 1984. The domestication of politics: Women and American political society, 1789–1920. *American Historical Review* 89: 620–647.

Ball, T. 1993. New faces of power. In T. Wartenberg (Ed.). *Rethinking power.* Albany: State University of New York Press.

Beck, L. 1994. *Reclaiming educational administration as a caring profession.* New York: Teachers College Press.

Beekley, C. 1996. Gender, expectations and job satisfaction: Why women exit the public school superintendency. Paper presented at the annual meeting of the American Educational Research Association, New York.

Belenky, M., G. Clinchy, N. Goldberger, and J. Tarule. 1986. *Women's ways of knowing: The development of self, voice, and mind.* New York: Basic Books.

Bell, C. 1988. Organizational influences on women's experience in the superintendency. *Peabody Journal of Education* 65 (4): 31–59.

Bell, C. 1995. "If I weren't involved with schools, I might be radical": Gender consciousness in context. In D. M Dunlop and P. A. Schnuck (Eds.). *Women leading in education*. Albany: State University of New York Press.

Bennis, W. 1989. *On becoming a leader*. New York: Addison-Wesley Publishing Company, Inc.

Bernard, J. 1973. My four revolutions: An autobiographical history of the American Sociological Society. *American Journal of Sociology 78*: 773–91.

Blumburg, A. 1985. *The school superintendent: Living with conflict*. New York: Teachers College Press.

Boals, K. 1975. The politics of male-female relations: The functions of feminist scholarship. *Signs 1*: 161–174.

Bogdan, R., and S. Biklen. 1992. *Qualitative research for education: An introduction and methods*. Boston: Allyn & Bacon.

Bohm, D., and F. D. Peat. 1987. *Science, order and creativity*. Toronto, New York, London, Sydney, Auckland: Bantam Books.

Bolinger, D. 1980. *Language the loaded weapon: The use and abuse of language today*. London: Longman.

Bolman, L., and T. Deal. 1991. *Reframing organizations*. San Francisco: Jossey-Bass.

Bossert, S., D. Dwyer, B. Rowan, and G. Lee. 1982. The instructional management role of the principal. *Educational Administration Quarterly 18* (3): 34–64.

Bredeson, P. V. 1988. Perspective on schools: metaphors and management in education. *The Journal of Educational Administration 26* (3): 293–310.

Bredeson, P., and R. Faber, 1994. What do superintendents mean when they say they are involved in curriculum and instruction? Paper presented at the American Educational Research Association, New Orleans, La.

Brown, J. S. 1970. Risk propensity in decision making: A comparison of business and public school administrators. *Administrative Science Quarterly 15* (4): 473–481.

Brown, G., and B. J. Irby. 1998. Getting the first school executive position. In B. J. Irby and G. Brown (Eds.). *Women leaders: Structuring success*. Dubuque: Kendall/Hunt Publishing Company.

Brunner, C. C. 1993. *By power defined: Women in the superintendency*. Unpublished doctoral dissertation, University of Kansas, Lawrence.

Brunner, C. C. 1995. By power defined: Women in the superintendency. *Edcational Considerations 22* (2): 21–26.

Brunner, C. C. 1998. Can power support an "ethic of care"? An examination of the professional practices of women superintendents. *Journal for a Just and Caring Education 4* (2): 142–175.

Brunner, C. C. 1998. Women superintendents: Strategies for success. *Journal of Educational Administration 36* (2): 160–182.

Brunner, C. C., and P. Shumaker. 1998. Power and gender in "New View Public Schools." *Policy Studies Journal 26* (1): 30–45.

Brunner, C. C. (Ed.). 1999. *Sacred dreams: Women and the superintendency.* Albany: State University of New York Press.

Cantor, D. W., and T. Bernay. 1992. *Women in power: The secrets of leadership.* New York: Houghton Mifflin Company.

Capra, F. 1975. *The Tao of physics.* Boston: Shambhala.

Capra, F. 1982. *The turning point.* New York: Simon & Schuster.

Capra, F. 1996. *The web of life.* New York: Anchor Books, Doubleday.

Carter, D. S. G., T. E. Glass, and S. M. Hord. 1993. *Selecting, preparing, and developing the school district superintendent.* Washington, D.C.: The Falmer Press.

Carter, G. R., and W. G. Cunningham, 1997. *The American school superintendent: Leading in an age of pressure.* San Francisco: Jossey-Bass Publishers.

Castaneda, C. 1967. *Journey to Ixtlan: The lessons of Don Juan.* New York: Washington Square Press.

Castaneda, C. (1974). *Tales of power.* New York: Simon & Schuster.

Castaneda, C. 1981. *The eagle's gift.* New York: Washington Square Press.

Castaneda, C. (1987). *The power of silence: Further lessons of Don Juan.* New York: Simon & Schuster.

Chase, S. 1995. *Ambiguous empowerment: The work narratives of women school superintendents.* Amherst: University of Massachusetts Press.

Clark, K. 1993. *Leonardo da Vinci.* London: Penguin Books.

Clegg, S. R. 1989. *Frameworks of power.* London: Sage Publications.

Collins, P. H. 1991. *Black feminist thought.* New York: Routledge.

Conrad, C. 1982. Grounded theory: An alternative approach to research in higher education. *The Review of Higher Education* 5(4): 259–269.

Crowson, R. L. 1992. *School-community relations under reform.* Berkeley: McCutchan.

Crum, T. 1994. Centering as a daily practice. In R. Fields (Ed.). *The awakened warrior,* 97–99. New York: G. P. Putnam's Sons.

Dahl, R. A. 1961. *Who governs?* New Haven: Yale University Press.

Darling-Hammond, L. 1984. Beyond the commission reports: The coming crisis in teaching (R-3177-RC). Santa Monica: Rand.

District Superintendents Committee on Women and Minority Administrators. June 1997. *Preliminary report and recommendations.* C. Fowler, The University of the State of New York, New York State Education Department.

Dormar, A. D. 1997. *Healing mind, healthy woman: Using the mind-body connection.* New York: Doubleday and Company, Inc.

Dunlap, D. M., and P. A. Schmuck. (Eds.). 1995. *Women leading in education.* Albany: State University of New York Press.

Edson, E. D. 1988. *Pushing the limits: The female administrative aspirant.* Albany: State University of New York Press.

Edson, S. K. 1995. Ten years later: Too little, too late? In D. M. Dunlop and P. A. Schmuck (Eds.). *Women leading in education*. Albany: State University of New York Press.

Edwards, C. P. 1975. Societal complexity and moral development: A Kenyan study. *Ethos* 3: 505–527.

Ekman, P. 1973. Cross cultural studies of facial express. In P. Ekman (Ed.). *Darwin and facial expression: A century of research in review*. New York: Academic Press.

Emmet, D. 1953–54. The concept of power. *Proceedings of the Aristotelian Society 54*. London.

Epstein, C. F. 1970. *Women's place: Options and limits in professional careers*. Berkeley and Los Angeles: University of California Press.

Estes, C. P. (1992). *Women who run with the wolves: Myths and stories of the wild woman archetype*. New York: Ballantine Books.

Faltico, G. J. 1969. The vocabulary of nonverbal communication in the psychological interview. Unpublished doctoral dissertation, University of California, Los Angeles.

Faludi, S. 1991. *Backlash: The undeclared war against American women*. New York: Doubleday.

Ferguson, K. E. 1984. *The feminist case against bureaucracy*. Philadelphia: Temple University Press.

Fields, R. 1994. *The awakened warrior: Living with courage, compassion, and discipline*. New York: G. P. Putnam's Sons.

Follett, M. P. 1942. *Creative experience*. New York: Longmans, Green and Co.

Foster, W. 1986. *Paradigms and promises: New approaches to educational administration*. Buffalo: Prometheus Books.

Foucault, M. 1977. *Discipline and punish*. New York: Vintage.

French, M. 1985. *Beyond power: On women, men, and morals*. London: Cape.

Frieze, I., J. E. Parsons, P. B. Johnson, D. N. Ruble, and G. L. Zellman. 1978. *Women and sex roles: A social psychological perspective*. New York: W. W. Norton and Company.

Gelb, M. J. 1998. *How to think like Leonardo da Vinci: Seven steps to genius every day*. New York: Delacorte Press.

Gilligan, C. 1982. *In a different voice: Psychological theory and women's development*. Cambridge: Harvard University Press.

Glaser, B. G., and A. L. Strauss. 1967. *The discovery of grounded theory: Behaviors for qualitative research*. New York: Aldine De Gruyter.

Gleick, J. 1987. *Chaos: Making a new science*. New York: Viking Penguin Inc.

Griffiths, D. E. 1966. *The school superintendent*. New York: Center for Applied Research in Education.

Grogan, M. 1996. *Voices of women aspiring to the superintendency*. Albany: State University of New York Press.

Grogan, M. 1998. Feminist approaches to educational leadership: Relationships based on care. In B. J. Irby and G. Brown (Eds.). *Women leaders: Structuring success*, 21–30. Dubuque: Kendall/Hunt Publishing Company.

Gross, N., W. S. Mason, and A. W. McEachen. 1958. *Explorations in role analysis: Studies of the school superintendency role*. New York: Wiley.

Guba, E., and Y. Lincoln. 1981. *Effective evaluation*. San Francisco: Jossey-Bass.

Gupton, S. L. 1998. Women as successful school superintendents. In B. J. Irby and G. Brown (Eds.). *Women leaders: Structuring success*, 180–189. Dubuque, Iowa: Kendall/Hunt Publishing Company.

Habermas, J. 1981. Hannah Arendt's communications concept of power. In S. Lukes (Ed.). *Power*. New York: New York University Press.

Hall, E. T. 1959. *The silent language*. Garden City: Doubleday.

Hartsock, N. 1981. Political change: Two perspectives on power. In C. Bunch (Ed.). *Building feminist theory: Essays from Quest*. New York: Longman.

Hartsock, N. 1983. *Money, sex, and power*. New York: Longman.

Hartsock, N. 1987. Foucault on power: A theory for women? In L. Nicholson (Ed.). *Feminism/postmodernism*. London: Routledge Press.

Haughland, M. 1987. Professional competencies needed by school superintendents, as perceived by school board members and superintendents in South Dakota. *ERS Spectrum 5* (4): 409–42.

Heilbrun, C. 1988. *Writing a woman's life*. New York: Ballantine Books.

Helsel, A. R., and S. P. Krchniak. 1972. Socialization in a heteronomous profession: Public school teaching. *The Journal of Educational Research 66* (2): 89–93.

Hennig, M., and J. Jardim. 1977. *The managerial woman*. New York: Anchor Press.

Herzog, K. 1986. *Foundation funding policy: A case study of philanthropic initiatives*. Unpublished doctoral dissertation, University of Kansas, Lawrence.

Hesselbein, F., M. Goldsmith, and R. Beckhard (Eds.). 1996. *The leader of the future: New visions, strategies, and practices for the next era*. San Francisco: Jossey-Bass Publishers.

Hill, M. S., and J. C. Ragland, 1995. *Women as educational leaders: Opening windows and pushing ceilings*. Thousands Oaks, Cal.: Corwin Press, Inc.

Hillman, J. 1994. Wars, arms, rams, mars: On the love of war. In Fields, R. (Ed.). *The awakened warrior: Living with courage, compassion, and discipline*, 70–88. New York: G. P. Putnam's Sons.

Holstein, C. 1976. Development of moral judgment: A longitudinal study of males and females. *Child Development 47*: 51–61.

Hughes Chapman, C. 1997. *Becoming a superintendent: Challenges of school district leadership*. Upper Saddle River, N.J.: Merrill.

Hunter, F. 1953. *Community power structure: A study of decision-makers*. Chapel Hill: University of North Carolina Press.

Immegart, G. L. 1988. Leadership and leader behavior. In N. J. Goyan (Ed.). *Handbook of research on educational administration*, 259–278. New York: Longman.

Issac, J. 1993. Beyond the three faces of power: A realist critique. In T. Wartenberg (Ed.). *Rethinking power*. Albany: State University of New York Press.

Josefowitz, N. 1980. *Paths to power: A woman's guide from first job to top executive*. London: Columbus.

Joseph, L. E. 1990. *Gaia: The growth of an idea*. New York: St. Martin's Press.

Kahn, R. L., D. M. Wolfe, R. P. Quinn, and J. D. Snoek. 1964. *Organizational stress: Studies in role conflict and ambiguity*. New York: Wiley.

Kanter, R. M. 1977. *Men and women of the corporation*. New York: Basic Books, Inc.

Kohlberg, L. 1958. *The development of modes of thinking and choices in years 10 to 16*. Unpublished doctoral dissertation, University of Chicago.

Kohlberg, L., and R. Kramer, 1969. Continuities and discontinuities in child and adult moral development. *Human Development 12*: 93–120.

Konnert, M. W., and J. J. Augenstein. 1990. *The superintendency in the nineties: What superintendents and board members need to know*. Lancaster, Pa.: Technomic Publishing Co., Inc.

Konnert, W., and J. B. Garner. Spring 1987. Assessing and altering risk-taking propensity: Keys to superintendency success. *Catalyst*: 7–12.

Kowalski, T. J. 1995. *Keepers of the flame: Contemporary urban superintendents*. Thousand Oaks, Cal.: Corwin Press, Inc.

Kozol, J. 1991. *Savage inequalities*. New York: HarperCollins.

Kuenne, R. E. 1993. *Economic justice in American society*. Princeton: Princeton University Press.

Ladson-Billings, G. 1995. Toward a theory of culturally relevant pedagogy. *American Educational Research Journal 32* (3): 465–491.

Lakoff, R. 1975. *Language and woman's place*. New York: Harper & Row.

Lakoff, G., and M. Johnson. 1980. *Metaphors we live by*. Chicago and London: The University of Chicago Press.

Lasswell, H. D., and A. Kaplan. 1950. *Power and society*. New Haven: Yale University Press.

Lather, P. 1991. *Getting smart: Feminist research and pedagogy with/in the postmodern*. New York and London: Routledge.

Leithwood, K. (Ed.). 1995. *Effective school district leadership: Transforming politics into education*. Albany: State University of New York Press.

Lincoln, Y. S., and E. G. Guba. 1985. *Naturalistic inquiry*. Beverly Hills: Sage.

Lindle, J. C. Spring 1993. A rhetorical legacy for leadership: Humor. *Educational Considerations 20* (2): 20–22.

Lindle, J. C. 1995. Needed: A knowledge base that promoted creativity—toward a rhetorical knowledge base for educational administration. In R. Donmoyer, M. Imber, and J. J. Scheurich (Eds.). *The knowledge base in educational administration: Multiple perspectives*, 257–266. Albany: The State University of New York Press.

Lowenthal, M. F., M. Thurnher, D. Chiriboga, and Associates. 1975. *Four stages of life: A comparative study of women and men facing transitions*. San Francisco: Jossey-Bass.

Lukes, S. 1974. *Power: A radical view*. London: The Macmillan Press, Ltd.

Lutz, F. W., and C. Mertz, 1992. *The politics of school/community relations*. New York and London: Teachers College Press.

Maccoby, E. E., and W. C. Wilson, 1957. Identification and observational learning from films. *Journal of Abnormal and Social Psychology 55*: 76–87.

Marshall, C. 1984. *Women managers: Travelers in a male world*. Chichester: Wiley.

Marshall, C. 1985. The stigmatized woman: The professional woman in a male sex-typed career. *Journal of Educational Administration 23* (2): 131–152.

Marshall, C. 1989. More than black face and skirts: New leadership to conform the major dilemmas in education. *Agenda 1* (4): 4–11.

Martinez, Z. N. 1988. From a representational to a holographic paradigm: The emergence of female power. *Atlantis 14*: 134–140.

May, R. 1975. *The courage to create*. New York: Bantam Books.

McCall, A. L. 1995. The bureaucratic restraints to caring in schools. In D. M. Dunlap and P. A. Schmuck (Eds.). *Women leaders in education*. Albany: State University of New York Press.

McGrew-Zoubi, R. 1993. Women's leadership style. In G. Brown and B. J. Irby (Eds.). *Women as school executives: A powerful paradigm*, 43–54. Huntsville, Tex.: Texas Council for women School Executives, Sam Houston Press.

Melendez, S. E. 1996. An "outsider's" view of leadership. In F. Hesselbein, M. Goldsmith, and R. Beckman (Eds.). *The leader of the future*. San Francisco: Jossey-Bass Publishers.

Meyer, M. April 1997. Laughter: It's good medicine. *Better Homes and Gardens*, 72–76.

Mier, R. 1993. *Social justice and local development policy*. Newbury Park, Cal.: Sage.

Miklos, E. 1988. Administrator selection, career patterns, succession, and socialization. In N. J. Boyan (Ed.). *Handbook of Research on Educational Administration*. New York: Longman.

Miles, M., and A. Huberman. 1984. *Qualitative data analysis*. Beverly Hills: Sage.

Mill, J. S. 1869. *Human mind*. Referenced by T. Wartenberg (1990). *The forms of power*, 18. Philadelphia: Temple University Press.

Miller, J. B. 1976. *Toward a new psychology of women*. Boston: Beacon Press.

Miller, J. B. 1993. Women and power. In T. Wartenberg (Ed.). *Rethinking power*. Albany: State University of New York Press.

Mladenka, K. 1980. The urban bureaucracy and the Chicago political machine: Who gets what and the limits of political control. *American Political Science Review 6* (1): 16.

Moore Johnson, S. 1996. *Leading to change: The challenge of the new superintendency.* San Francisco: Jossey-Bass Publishers.

Moore-Johnson, S. 1996. *Leading to change.* San Francisco: Jossey Bass.

Morgan, G. 1993. *Imaginization: The art of creative management.* Newbury Park, Cal.: Sage Publications.

Murphy, J. 1988. Methodological, measurement, and conceptual problems in the study of instructional leadership. *Educational Evaluation and Policy Analysis 10* (2): 117–139.

Nagel, J. 1975. *The descriptive analysis of power.* New Haven: Yale University Press.

New York State Education Department, BEDS Data, 1995–1996; 1997.

Noddings, N. 1984. *Caring: A feminine approach to ethics and moral education.* Los Angeles: University of California Press.

Noddings, N. 1992. *The challenge to care in schools: An alternative approach to education.* New York: Teachers College Press.

Norton, M. S., L. D. Webb, L. L. Dlugosh, and W. Sybouts. 1996. *The school superintendency: New responsibilities, new leadership.* Needham Heights, Mass.: Allyn & Bacon.

Okin, S. 1989. *Justice, gender, and the family.* New York: Basic Books.

Olderman, R. M. 1995. *Alien information: The experience of insight and its influence on America after 1970.* Unpublished manuscript.

Olsen, T. 1978. *Silences.* New York: Delacorte Press.

Ortiz, F. I. 1982. *Career paths in education: Women, men, and minorities in public school administration.* New York: Praeger.

Papenek, H. 1973. Men, women, and work: Reflections on the two-person career. In J. Huber (Ed.). *Changing women in a changing society.* Chicago: University of Chicago Press.

Patton, M. Q. 1980. *Qualitative evaluation methods.* Beverly Hills: Sage.

Pitkin, H. 1972. *Wittgenstein and justice.* Berkeley: University of California Press.

Polsby, N. W. 1980. *Community power and political theory.* New Haven: Yale University Press.

Pounder, D. 1994. Educational and demographic trends: Implications for women's representation in school administration. In P. Thurston and N. Prestine (Eds.). *Advanced in educational administration,* Vol III, 135–149. Greenwich, Ct.: JAI Press.

Pounder, D. (Ed.). 1998. *Restructuring schools for collaboration: Promises and pitfalls.* Albany: State University of New York Press.

Powell, R. E. 1984. A comparison of selection criteria and performance evaluation criteria for Missouri school superintendents. Unpublished doctoral dissertation, University of Missouri-Columbia.

Purpel, D. E. 1989. *The moral and spiritual crisis in education: A curriculum for justice and compassion in education.* New York: Bergin & Garvey.

Radloff, L. 1975. Sex differences in depression: The effects of occupation and marital status. *Sex Roles 1* (3): 249–265.

Raines, R. A. 1973. *To kiss the joy.* Waco: Word Books, Publisher.

Raymond, J. 1986. *A passion for friends: Towards a philosophy of female affection.* London: Women's Press.

Regan, H. B., and G. H. Brooks. 1995. *Out of women's experience: Creating relational leadership.* Thousand Oaks, Cal.: Corwin Press.

Rich, A. 1979. *On lies, secrets, and silence: Selected prose 1966–1978.* New York: W. W. Norton.

Robertson, M. C. 1984. A survey of the selection of school superintendent in Massachusetts. Unpublished doctoral dissertation, Boston University.

Robinson, J. R., and P. E. Converse. (May 30, 1966). *Summary of the U. S. time use survey.*

Russell, B. 1938. *Power: A new social analysis.* London: Allen and Unwin.

Russell, B. 1975. The forms of power. In S. Lukes (Ed.). *Power,* 19–27. Albany: State University of New York Press.

Sarason, D. B. 1990. *The predictable failure of educational reform: Can we change course before it's too late?* San Francisco: Jossey-Bass Publications.

Schmuck, P. 1975. *Sex differentiation in public school administration.* American Arlington, Va.: Association of School Administrators.

Schmuck, P. A. 1982. *Women educators: Employees of schools in western countries.* Albany: State University of New York Press.

Schmuck, P. 1995. Advocacy organizations for women school administrators, 1977–1993. In D. M. Dunlop and P. A. Schmuck (Eds.). *Women leading in education.* Albany: State University of New York Press.

Schmuck, P. A., and J. Schubert. 1995. Women principals' views on sex equity: Exploring issues of integration and information. In D. M. Dunlop and P. A. Schmuck (Eds.). *Women leading in education.* Albany: State University of New York Press.

Schlozman, K. L., Burns, N., Verba, S., and J. Donahue. 1995. Gender and citizen participation: Is there a different voice? *American Journal of Political Science,* 39, 267–293.

Schumaker, P. 1991. *Critical pluralism.* Lawrence: University Press of Kansas.

Sclafani, S. 1987. AASA guidelines for preparation of school administrators: Do they represent the important job behaviors of superintendents? Doctoral dissertation, Austin, University of Texas.

Sergiovanni, T. J. 1994. *Building community in schools.* San Francisco: Jossey-Bass.

Shakeshaft, C. 1989. *Women in educational administration.* Newbury Park: Sage Publications.

Simon, H. A. 1953. Notes on the observation and measurement of power. *Journal of Politics 15*: 500–516.

Simpson, E. L. 1974. Moral development research: A case study of scientific cultural bias. *Human Development 17*: 81–106.

Singer, L. 1987. Value, power, and gender: Do we need a different voice? In J. Genova (Ed.). *Power, gender, values*. Edmonton, Alberta: Academic Press.

Skrtic, T. 1985. Doing naturalistic research into educational organizations. In Lincoln, Y. S. (Ed.). *Organizational theory and inquiry: The paradigm revolution*. Beverly Hills: Sage.

Spelman, E. 1988. *Inessential woman*. Boston: Beacon Press.

Steinem, G. 1994. *Moving beyond words: Breaking boundaries of gender*. New York: Simon & Schuster.

Stone, C. 1980. Systemic power in community decision making. *American Political Science Review* 74: 978–990.

Stone, C. 1989. *Regime politics*. Lawrence: University Press of Kansas.

Strauss, A. 1987. *Qualitative analysis for social scientists*. New York: Cambridge University Press.

Tallerico, M. 1999. Women and the superintendency: What do we really know? In C. C. Brunner (Ed.). *Sacred dreams: Women and the superintendency*. Albany: State University of New York Press.

Tallerico, M., and J. N. Burstyn. 1996. Retaining women in the superintendency: The location matters. *Educational Administration Quarterly* 32: 642–664.

Tallerico, M., J. N. Burstyn, and W. Poole. 1993. *Gender and politics at work: Why women exit the superintendency*. Fairfax, Va.: National Policy Board for Educational Administration.

Tannen, D. 1986. *That's not what I meant! How conversational style makes or breaks relationships*. New York: Ballantine Books.

Tannen, D. 1990. *You just don't understand: Women and men in conversation*. New York: Ballantine Books.

Tannen, D. 1994. *Gender and discourse*. New York, Oxford: Oxford University Press.

Tannen, D. 1995. *Talking from 9 to 5: Women and men in the workplace: Language, sex, and power*. New York: Avon Books.

Tronto, J. 1994. *Moral boundaries: A political argument for the ethic of care*. New York: Routledge.

Tyack, D., and E. Hansot, 1982. *Managers of virtue: Public school leadership in America, 1820–1980*. New York: Basic Books.

Vanello, M., and R. Siemienska. 1990. *Gender inequality: A comparative study of discrimination and participation*. Sage Studies in International Sociology.

Vega, M. 1994. The warrioress creed. In Fields, R. (Ed.). *The awakened warrior: Living with courage, compassion, and discipline*, 89. New York: G. P. Putnam's Sons.

Wartenberg, T. E. 1990. *The forms of power: From domination to transformation*. Philadelphia: Temple University Press.

Weber, M. [1924] 1947. *The theory of social and economic organizations*. A. H. Henderson & T. Parsons (Eds.). Glencoe, Ill.: Free Press. (first published in 1924).

Weiler, K. 1988. *Women teaching for change*. New York: Bergin & Garvey.

Welwood, J. 1994. The warriors of the heart. In Fields, R. (Ed.). *The awakened warrior: Living with courage, compassion, and discipline*, 99–101. New York: G. P. Putnam's Sons.

Wheatley, M. J. 1992. *Leadership and the new science: Learning about organization from an orderly universe*. San Francisco: Brett-Koehler Publishers, Inc.

Whyte, W. H. 1956. *The organization man*. New York: Simon and Schuster.

Winfield, L. F. 1997. Multiple dimensions of reality: Recollections of an African American woman scholar. In A. Neumann and P. L. Peterson (Eds.). *Learning from our lives: Women, research, and autobiography in education*, 194–208. New York and London: Teachers College Press.

Wolfe, N. 1994. *Fire with fire: The new female power and how to use it*. New York: Fawcett Columbine.

INDEX